Briefing

the

BIBLE

Outlines of Each Book of the Bible
to Encourage Reading Through the Bible

by

J. Vernon McGee

Thru the Bible Books
P. O. Box 100
Pasadena, California 91109

Reprinted 1978

Printed by
El Camino Press
La Verne, Calif.

CONTENTS
(Alphabetical List)

CONTENTS

The Old Testament

The New Testament

WHEN YOU READ THE BIBLE THROUGH

I supposed I knew my Bible,
  Reading piecemeal, hit or miss,
Now a bit of John or Matthew,
  Now a snatch of Genesis,
Certain chapter of Isaiah,
  Certain Psalms (the twenty-third),
Twelfth of Romans, First of Proverbs—
  Yes, I thought I knew the Word!
But I found that thorough reading
  Was a different thing to do,
And the way was unfamiliar
  When I read the Bible through.
You who like to play at Bible,
  Dip and dabble, here and there,
Just before you kneel, aweary,
  And yawn through a hurried prayer;
You who treat the Crown of Writings
  As you treat no other book—
Just a paragraph disjointed,
  Just a crude impatient look—
Try a worthier procedure,
  Try a broad and steady view;
You will kneel in very rapture
  When you read the Bible through!

        —Amos R. Wells

The first five books of the Bible are called the Pentateuch. Pentateuch means five books. These books were written by Moses, and are identified in Scripture as the Law. Although the Mosaic authorship has been questioned, it is affirmed by conservative scholars and confirmed by archaeology. Bible believers unanimously accept the Mosaic authorship (Deut. 31:9, 24-26; Acts 7:37, 38).

GENESIS

"The Seed Plot of the Bible"

WRITER: Moses

NAME: Genesis

The name *Genesis* is taken from the Septuagint. The Septuagint (LXX) is a Greek translation made of the Old Testament in Alexandria at the order of Ptolemy Philadelphus about 285-247 B.C. Josephus tells us that this translation was made by 72 priests (hence its name) in 72 days. Six priests were from each of the 12 tribes. Christ and Paul quoted from this translation of the Old Testament. It is older than any of the Hebrew texts extant today.

Genesis is the book of beginnings and the families—the beginning of creation, man, woman, sabbath, marriage, family, work, sin, murder, sacrifice, races, languages, culture, civilization and redemption.

Genesis means "origin," "source," "birth." The meaning closest to that of the original is "birth." It is derived from the Greek verb *gennao,* which means to beget or give birth to. Genesis is the book of beginnings and sources, but more particularly it is the book of births—this is often overlooked. It is the book of generations. According to this understanding of Genesis, it falls into two natural divisions:

Genesis

1. Gen 2:4—The Book of the Birth of Heaven and the Earth (from Septuagint)
2. Gen 5:1—The Book of the Birth of Men

Simply stated, the book of Genesis is the record of the "family tree" of the Jews. It is the genealogy of heaven, earth, and man. Even the new birth is suggested in Genesis 3:15, where is the first mention of a Redeemer.

OUTLINE (According to Genealogies):

Gen. 1-2:6	Book of Generations of Heavens and Earth —Divine Poem of Creation—God's Creative Work
Gen. 2:7-6:8	Book of Generations of Adam (men, *anthropoi*). Adam Created but Children Born to Him
Gen. 6:9-9:29	Generations of Noah
Gen. 10:1-11:9	Generations of Sons of Noah
Gen. 11:10-26	Generations of Sons of Shem (Gentiles)
Gen. 11:27-25:11	Generations of Terah
Gen. 25:12-18	Generations of Ishmael
Gen. 25:19-35:29	Generations of Isaac (why Abraham left out, "In Isaac shall thy seed be called" cf. Gen. 21:12; Heb. 11:8; Rom. 9:7)
Gen. 36:1-37:1	Generations of Esau
Gen. 37:2-50:26	Generations of Jacob (genealogy of rejected line given first, chosen line last, cf. 1 Cor. 15:46 for principle in giving genealogies)

KEY: Generations

PURPOSE: To give us the families—Gen. 12:3; 22:18; 28:13, 14; Acts 3:25; Gal. 3:6, 9, 16

The first 11 chapters cover a minimum of 2000 years. It could easily be a thousand times longer. From chapter 12 to chapter 50 the time is 350 years. This should arrest our attention.

11 chapters cover 2000 years, plus.
39 chapters cover only 350 years.

Certainly the record slows down at chapter 12. Better stated, the first 11 chapters constitute an introduction to the remainder of the book and the Bible. This chart may prove helpful.

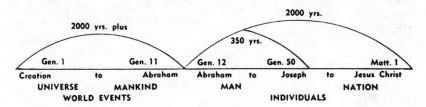

Abraham is more important to God than the universe. It is only being fair to an author to place the emphasis where he places it.

In the New Testament God indicates emphasis in the same way. The four Gospels record the main events in the life of Jesus Christ. Examine the following facts:

There are 89 chapters in the 4 Gospels. Of these
4 chapters cover the first 30 years of His life,
85 chapters cover the last 3 years of His life,
27 chapters cover the last 8 days of His life.

Which is more important to the writers, judging from the space given to each—the first 30 years or the last 8 days? Four chapters cover the first 30 years and 27 chapters cover the last 8 days. When you turn to the Epistles, you discover why the emphasis is on the death, burial, and resurrection of the Lord Jesus Christ (1 Cor. 15:1-4). These facts constitute the Gospel; your salvation rests upon them. Do you believe that Jesus Christ died for your sins, and that He was raised for your justification? This is essential.

One of the harshest and most frequently heard criticisms of the Bible concerns the creation account. It is pointed out that other nations of antiquity had such a story. This is true, but a comparison of the Genesis record with one of the best of a secular nation, the Babylonian tablets of creation, will show the superiority of the Genesis record. Here all is contrast:

Babylonian	*Bible*
Tablets begin with chaos	Bible begins with cosmos, perfection

Genesis

Babylonian	Bible
Heavenly bodies are gods	Heavenly bodies are matter
Polytheistic theology (many gods)	Monotheistic truth (one God)
Work of a craftsman	God spoke
Characterized by puerility and grotesqueness	Grand and solemn realities of the Creator God who is holy and who is a Saviour
Out of harmony with science	In accord with science (many scientists are believers)

OUTLINE

A. Entrance of Sin on Earth, chs. 1-11
  I. **Creation, chs. 1, 2**
    1. Heaven and Earth, 1:1
      "Create" (bara) occurs only 3 times, vv. 1, 21, 27.
    2. Earth Became Waste and Void, 1:2
    3. Re-creation, 1:3-2:25
      (1) First Day—Light, 1:3-5
      (2) Second Day—Air Spaces (Firmament), 1:6-8
      (3) Third Day—Dry Land Appears and Plant Life, 1:9-13
      (4) Fourth Day—Sun, Moon, Stars Appear 1:14-19
      (5) Fifth Day—Animal Life (Biology), 1:20-23
      (6) Sixth Day—Fertility of Creation and Creation of Man, 1:24-31
      (7) Seventh Day—Sabbath, 2:1-3
      (8) Recapitulation of the Creation of Man, 2:4-25 *(law of recurrence)*

  II. **Fall, chs. 3, 4**
    1. Root of Sin—Doubting and Disobeying God
    2. Fruit of Sin—
      "Out of the heart proceed...murders..." (Matt. 15:19)

  III. **Flood** (deluge), **chs. 5-9**
    1. Book of Generations of Adam—Through Seth Beginning of Man's History—Obituary Notices, ch. 5
    2. Antediluvian Civilization— Cause of Flood and Construction of Ark, ch. 6
    3. Judgment of Flood, ch. 7
    4. Postdiluvian Civilization—After the Flood, ch. 8
    5. Postdiluvian Life—New Beginning, ch. 9

IV. **Tower of Babel and Confusion of Tongues, chs. 10, 11**
   1. Ethnology—Sons of Noah, ch. 10
   2. Tower of Babel, ch. 11
   (contrast to Day of Pentecost)

B. Preparation for the Coming of the Redeemer of All Mankind, chs. 12-50
   I. **Abraham** (faith), **chs. 12-23**
   (development of faith by 7 appearances of God)
   1. God's Call and Promise to Abram—
      His Response by Lapse of Faith, ch. 12
   2. Abram Returns to Land from Egypt—Separates from Lot
      God Then Appears the Third Time to Abraham, ch. 13
   3. The First War—Abram Delivers Lot
      The First Priest—Abram Blessed by Melchizedek, ch. 14
   4. God Reveals Himself More Completely
      to Abram—Reaffirms His Promises, ch. 15
   5. Unbelief of Sarai and Abram—Birth of Ishmael, ch. 16
   6. God Makes Covenant with Abraham
      (Abram Becomes Abraham)
      Confirms Promise to Abraham About a Son, ch. 17
   7. God Reveals Coming Destruction of Sodom to Abraham—
      Abraham Intercedes on Behalf of Inhabitants, ch. 18
   8. Angels Warn Lot—Lot Leaves Sodom—
      God Destroys Cities of the Plain, ch. 19
   9. Abraham Repeats Sin
      at Gerar About Relationship of Sarah, ch. 20
   10. Birth of Isaac—Hagar and Ishmael Cast Out—
       Abraham at Beer-sheba, ch. 21
   11. God Commands Abraham to Offer Isaac—Restrains Him—
       Reconfirms Covenant with Abraham, ch. 22
   12. Death of Sarah—Abraham Purchases
       Machpelah Cave for Burial Place, ch. 23

   II. **Isaac** (the Beloved Son), **chs. 24-26**
   Choosing of a bride compares with Christ and the Church.
   1. Abraham Sends Servant for Bride for Isaac—
      Rebekah Returns With Him—Becomes Isaac's Bride, ch. 24
   2. Death of Abraham—Birth of Esau and Jacob (twins) to
      Isaac and Rebekah—Esau Sells Birthright to Jacob, ch. 25
   3. God confirms Covenant to Isaac—Isaac Misrepresents
      Relationship with Rebekah—Isaac Digs Well in Gerar, ch. 26

III. **Jacob** *"Whom the Lord loveth He chasteneth",* **chs. 27-36**
  1. Jacob and Rebekah Connive
     to Get Blessing Intended for Esau, ch. 27
  2. Jacob Leaves Home—At Bethel God Appears to Him—
     Confirms Abrahamic Covenant, ch. 28
  3. Jacob Arrives in Haran—Meets Rachel and Uncle Laban—
     Serves for Rachel—Deceived into Marrying Leah, ch. 29
  4. Birth of Sons to Jacob—Jacob Prepares to Leave Laban—
     Jacob's Bargain Pays Off, ch. 30
  5. Jacob Flees from Haran—Laban Overtakes Him—
     Jacob and Laban Make Mizpah Covenant, ch. 31
  6. Crisis in Life of Jacob: At Peniel a Man Wrestles with
     Him—Jacob's Name Changed to Israel, ch. 32
  7. Jacob Meets Esau—Jacob Journeys to Shalem, ch. 33
  8. Scandal in Jacob's Family: Dinah Defiled—Brothers
     Avenge by Slaying Men of Hamor, ch. 34
  9. Jacob Returns to Bethel—Rachel Dies at Bethlehem
     —Isaac Dies at Hebron, ch. 35
  10. Family of Esau Which Becomes Nation of Edom, ch. 36

IV. **Joseph** *(suffering and glory),* **chs. 37-50**
  1. Jacob Dwells in Canaan—Joseph Sold Into Slavery, ch. 37
  2. Sin and Shame of Judah, ch. 38
  3. Humiliation in Egypt, chs. 39, 40
     (1) Overseer in House of Potiphar—
         Tempted then Framed
         by Wife of Potiphar—Imprisoned, ch. 39
     (2) Joseph in Prison
         Interprets Dreams of Baker and Butler, ch. 40
  4. Exaltation in Egypt, chs. 41-48
     (1) Joseph Interprets Dreams of Pharoah—
         Made Overseer of Egypt—Marries Asenath—
         Birth of Manasseh and Ephraim, ch. 41
     (2) Jacob Sends 10 Sons to Egypt for Corn—Audience
         with Joseph—Leave Simeon as Hostage—Return
         Home with Corn and Refunded Money, ch. 42
     (3) Jacob Sends Sons (Benjamin Included) Again to
         Egypt—Entertained in Joseph's Home
         (Does Not Reveal His Identity), ch. 43
     (4) Joseph Sends Brothers Home—Arrested by Steward—
         Cup Found in Benjamin's Sack—
         Judah Pleads for Benjamin, ch. 44

(5) Joseph Reveals Identity—
Tender Reunion with Brothers—
Invites Jacob and All Family to Egypt, ch. 45
(6) Jacob with Family (70) Move to Egypt—
Jacob and Joseph Reunited, ch. 46
(7) Jacob and Brothers Dwell in Goshen—Presented to
Pharaoh—Famine Forces Egyptians to Sell Land to
Joseph for Pharaoh—Joseph Swears He Will Bury
Jacob in Canaan, ch. 47
(8) Jacob on Deathbed Blesses Joseph's Sons, ch. 48
5. Death and Burial of Jacob and Joseph, chs. 49, 50
(1) Jacob Gives Deathbed Blessing
and Prophecy for 12 Sons, ch. 49
(2) Death and Burial of Jacob in Canaan—
Death and Burial of Joseph in Egypt, ch. 50

RECOMMENDED BOOKS FOR FURTHER STUDY:

Boyd, Eleanor H.: *The Gospel in Genesis.*
Candlish, Robert S.: *Commentary on Genesis* (2 volumes).
Gray, James J.: *Synthetic Bible Studies.* Fleming H. Revell Co.,
Westwood, N.J.
Lange, John Peter.: *Genesis.*
Leupold, H. C.: *Exposition of Genesis* (2 volumes).
Baker Book House, Grand Rapids, Michigan.
Mackintosh, C. H.: *Notes on Genesis.* Loizeaux Brothers, Inc.,
New York, N.Y.
Moorehead, W. G.: *Outline Studies in the Books of the Old
Testament.*
Pink, Arthur W.: *Gleanings in Genesis.* Moody Press, Chicago,
Illinois.
Ridout, Samuel: *The Pentateuch.*
Scofield, C. I.: *Bible Correspondence Course,* Vol. 1.
Thomas, W. H. Griffith: *Genesis.* Wm. B. Eerdmans Publishing
Co., Grand Rapids, Michigan.
Turnbull, M. R.: *Studying the Book of Genesis.*

EXODUS

WRITER:

Moses (see outline of Genesis)

A CONTINUED STORY:

Exodus continues the account which was begun in Genesis, although there was a lapse of at least 3½ centuries. Genesis 15:13 says that the seed of Abraham would spend 400 years in Egypt. Exodus 12:40 says that it was 430 years, and Galatians 3:16, 17 confirms it. It was 430 years from the call of Abraham, and 400 years from the time that God told Abraham. It is difficult to be dogmatic about the chronology of the partriarchal period. It has been omitted purposely from these outlines. The word which opens Exodus is a conjunction which is better translated "and" rather than "now." Exodus has been called the sequel to Genesis. Dr. G. Campbell Morgan wrote, "In the book of Exodus nothing is commenced, nothing is finished."

MESSAGE:

Exodus means "the way out." Redemption is by blood and by power. The message is stated in Hebrews 11:23-29.

KEY VERSE: Ex. 20:2

OUTLINE:

I. A Deliverer, chs. 1-11

    1. Slavery of Israel in Egypt, ch. 1

    2. Birth of Moses—First 40 Years in Pharaoh's Palace, ch. 2

    3. Call of Moses—Second 40 Years in Midian, ch. 3 (Incident of Burning Bush)

    4. Return of Moses to Egypt—Announcement of Deliverance to Israel, ch. 4

5. Contest with Pharaoh, chs. 5-11
   (9 Plagues against Idolatry of Egypt, Battle of the Gods)

II. Deliverance (by Blood and Power), **chs. 12-14**

1. Institution of Passover—Tenth Plague, Death of First-Born (Blood), ch. 12

2. Crossing Red Sea—Destruction of Army of Egypt (Power), chs. 13-14

III. Marching to Mt. Sinai (Spiritual Education), **chs. 15-18**
(7 experiences correspond to Christian experience)

1. Song of Redeemed—Wilderness of Shur, 15:1-22
   (no bed of roses after redemption)

2. Marah, Bitter Water Sweetened by Tree, 15:23-26
   (Cross sweetens bitter experiences of life.)

3. Elim *(fruitful Christian experience)*, 15:27

4. Wilderness of Sin—Manna and Quail, ch. 16
   (Christ is the Bread of life.)

5. Smitten Rock ("That Rock was Christ."), 17:1-7

6. Amalek *(the flesh)*, 17:8-16
   (victory on the hill top, Deut. 25:17, 18)

7. Jethro, Priest of Midian, ch. 18
   (worldly wisdom in contrast to revelation)

IV. The Law (Condemnation), **chs. 19-24**

1. Arrival at Mt. Sinai—
   Agreement to Accept the Law, ch. 19

2. 10 Commandments—Order for the Altar, ch. 20

3. Social Legislation, chs. 21-24

Exodus

V. Blueprint and Construction of Tabernacle, chs. 25-40
(a pattern and picture of Christ)

1. Blueprint for Tabernacle—Pattern of Garments for High Priest, chs. 25-30

2. Workmen for Tabernacle—
   Sabbath a Sign to Israel, ch. 31

3. Golden Calf—Broken Law—Moses' Intercession Second Tables of the Law, chs. 32-35

4. Construction of Tabernacle, chs. 36-39

5. Tabernacle Erected—Filled with Glory of the Lord, ch. 40

(Exodus Begins in Gloom and Ends in Glory)

RECOMMENDED BOOKS:

(See Genesis list.)

Boyd, Eleanor H.: *The Gospel in Exodus.*
Exell, Joseph S.: *The Biblical Illustrator, Exodus.*
Grant, F. W.: *Lessons from the Book of Exodus*
Mackintosh, C. H.: *Notes on Exodus.* Loizeaux Brothers, Inc., New York, N.Y.
Pfeiffer, Charles F.: *Egypt and the Exodus.* Baker Book House, Grand Rapids, Mich.
Pink, Arthur W.: *Gleanings in Exodus.* Moody Press, Chicago, Ill.

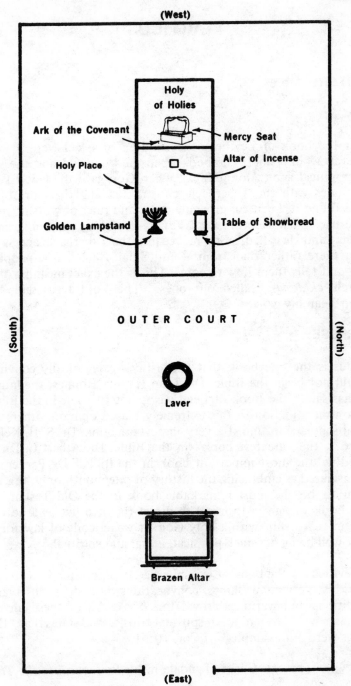

(West)

Holy
of Holies

Ark of the Covenant

Mercy Seat

Holy Place

Altar of Incense

Golden Lampstand

Table of Showbread

OUTER COURT

(South)

(North)

Laver

Brazen Altar

(East)

LEVITICUS

WRITER: Moses

PLACE:

In the book of Leviticus the children of Israel were marking time at Mount Sinai. The book opens and concludes at the same geographical spot, Mount Sinai, where God gave the law. Exodus concludes with the Tabernacle constructed and the glory of the Lord filling it. Leviticus gives the order and rules of worship in the Tabernacle. The Hebrew word *Vayick-rah* opens the book, and it means "and He called." God moves into the Tabernacle and speaks from there rather than from Mount Sinai. He calls the people to Him and tells them how to come. This is the exact meaning of the church—*ekklesia,* "called out ones." The Lord Jesus said, "My sheep hear my voice."

PURPOSE:

This is the one book that the critic is categorically convinced should not be in the Bible. Dr. John Haynes Holmes, the humanist, has said, "the Book of Leviticus is not fit to be in the Bible." In contradistinction to this extremely biased opinion, others with equal scholarship find it a very important book. Dr. S. H. Kellogg called it the "greatest book" in the Bible. Dr. Albert C. Dudley called it "the most important book in the Bible." Dr. Parker said, "Considered as embracing the history of one month only, this may claim to be the most remarkable book in the Old Testament." This book was given to Israel to direct them to live as a holy nation in fellowship with a holy God. It was a code of law for the total well-being of Israel, physical, moral and spiritual.

Leviticus is the book of worship. Sacrifice, ceremony, ritual, liturgy, instructions, washings, convocations, holy days, observances, conditions and warnings crowd this book. All of these physical exercises were given to teach spiritual truths. Paul states that "these things were our examples" [I Cor. 10:6].

Leviticus reveals Christ. Tyndale in his *Prologue into the Third*

Book of Moses, said, "Though sacrifices and ceremonies can be no ground or foundation to build upon—that is, though we can prove nought with them—yet when we have once found Christ and his mysteries, then we may borrow figures, that is to say, allegories similitudes, and examples, to open Christ, and the secrets of God hid in Christ, even unto the quick: and can declare them more lively and sensibly with them than with all the words in the world."

For us it gives the direction to God and instructions for spiritual worship. Worship would take on a new meaning if the average Christian properly appreciated the contents of this book.

KEY: Holiness to Jehovah

MESSAGE: The message is twofold.

1. Leviticus teaches that the **way to God is by sacrifice.** The word *atonement* occurs 45 times.

2. Leviticus teaches that the **walk with God is by sanctification.** The word *holiness* occurs 87 times.

OUTLINE

I. The **FIVE OFFERINGS** and the Law of Them, **chs. 1-7**

   A. **Sweet Savor** Offerings (Person of Christ), chs. 1-3

      1. **Burnt** Offering (Christ Our Substitute), ch. 1

      2. **Meal** Offering (Loveliness of Christ), ch. 2

      3. **Peace** Offering (Christ Our Peace), ch. 3

   B. **Non-Sweet Savor** Offerings
     (Work of Christ on Cross), chs. 4, 5

      1. **Sin** Offering (Sin as a Nature), ch. 4

      2. **Trespass** Offering (Sin as an Act), ch. 5

   C. Law of the Offerings, chs. 6, 7

Leviticus

II. The **PRIESTS** (All Believers Are Priests), **chs. 8-10**

A. **Consecration** of Priests, ch. 8

B. **Ministry** of Priests, ch. 9

C. **Restrictions** on Priests (Death of Nadab and Abihu), ch. 10

III. HOLINESS in Daily Life (God Concerned with His Children's Conduct), **chs. 11-22**

A. **Food** of God's People, ch. 11

B. **Children** of God's Children, ch. 12

C. Cleansing of **Leprosy,** chs. 13, 14

D. Cleansing of **Running Issues,** ch. 15

E. Great Day of **Atonement,** ch. 16

F. Place of Sacrifice; Value of the Blood, ch. 17

G. Application of **Commandments** to Life Situations, chs. 18-20

   1. **Immorality** Condemned (Amplification of 7th Commandment), ch. 18

   2. **Social Sins** (Application of Commandments), ch. 19

   3. **Penalty** for Breaking Commandments, ch. 20

H. Law for **Personal Purity** of Priests, chs. 21, 22 ·

IV. The **HOLY HOLIDAYS, ch. 23**

V. LAWS and **PROPHECIES** for the Promised Land, **chs. 24-26**

A. Lampstand, Showbread and Death Penalty for the Blasphemer, ch. 24

B. Sabbatic Year, Year of Jubilee
and Law of Kinsman Redeemer, ch. 25

C. Conditions of Blessing in the Land
(a Prophetic History), ch. 26

VI. Dedication and Devotion—Concerning **VOWS, ch. 27**

RECOMMENDED BOOKS FOR FURTHER STUDY:
(See Genesis)

Bonar, Andrew A.: *A Commentary on the Book of Leviticus.*
Boyd, Eleanor Herr: *The Gospel in Leviticus.*
Heslop, W. G.: *Lessons from Leviticus.*
Jellie, W. Harvey: *The Preacher's Commentary of the Book of Leviticus.*
Kellogg, S. H.: *The Book of Leviticus.*
Mackintosh, C. H.: *The Book of Leviticus.*

NUMBERS

(Called *Arithmoi* in the Septuagint, meaning "Arithmetic")

THEME: "PILGRIM'S PROGRESS"—walking, wandering, working, warring, witnessing and worshipping. It is a handbook for pilgrims. "Chart and compass come from Thee." It is a road map for the wilderness of this world.

> For whatever things were written in earlier times were written for our learning, that we, through patience and comfort of the scriptures, might have hope [Rom. 15:4].

> Now all these things happened unto them for examples, and they are written for our admonition, upon whom the ends of the ages are come [I Cor. 10:11].

> These all died in faith, not having received the promises but having seen them afar off, and were persuaded of them, and embraced them, and confessed that they were strangers and pilgrims on the earth [Heb. 11:13].

> Dearly beloved, I beseech you as sojourners and pilgrims, abstain from fleshly lusts which war against the soul [I Pet. 2:11].

> I have given them thy word, and the world hath hated them, because they are not of the world, even as I am not of the world. I pray not that thou shouldest take them out of the world, but that thou shouldest keep them from the evil [John 17:14, 15].

WRITER: Moses (see outline of Genesis)

FORWARD MARCH !

In the book of Numbers we see the children of Israel depart from Mt. Sinai and march to Kadesh-barnea. At Kadesh-barnea the attitude of unbelief is crystallized into actual disobedience. The light is focused on faith, and they failed. "So we see that they could not enter in because of unbelief" (Heb. 3:19). After Kadesh-barnea they began to wander until that entire generation died in the wilderness (two notable exceptions were Joshua and Caleb)

The years of wandering were a veritable saga of suffering, a trek of tragedy, and a story of straying.

Numbers gets its name from the census in the first chapter and the one in the twenty-sixth chapter. C.H.M. called it "a divine history of the wanderings of the Israelites in the wilderness for about 38 years and 10 months, commencing with the first movement of the camp after the tabernacle was reared."

KEY: 14:29-31

These verses outline the experiences of the children of Israel during the time of wandering until the new generation came to the east bank of the Jordan in the land of Moab.

HOW ISRAEL ENCAMPED ON WILDERNESS MARCH
CHART OF CAMP

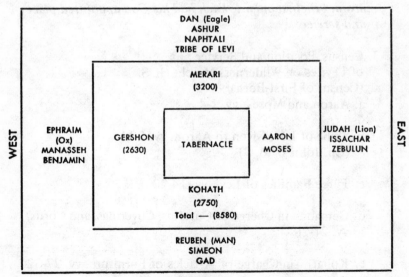

OUTLINE:

I. FITTING Out the Nation Israel for Wilderness March, chs. 1-8
(Preparation for the Pilgrimage)

A. Order of the Camp, chs. 1-4
"Let everything be done...in order"

  1. First Census, ch. 1

*(603,550 of those able to go to war [v.46]
Probably 2½ million came out of Egypt.)*

*An Israelite must be able to declare his pedigree,
know who he is in order to serve and fight.
A Christian must know his pedigree—"Now are
we the sons of God."*

  2. Standards and Position
of 12 Tribes on Wilderness March, ch. 2

*They must know where they belong (see chart), and rally
around their standard. Each had his God-appointed place
and service.*

  3. Census, Position and Service
of Levites on Wilderness March, ch. 3
(Census of First-Born)
a. Aaron and Moses, vv. 1-4

   b. Tribe of Levi Given to Aaron, vv. 5-13
(Cp. John 17:6, 9)

   c. Three Families of Levi, vv. 14-20

   d. Gershon—in Charge of Curtains, Coverings, and Cords,
vv. 21-26

   e. Kohath—in Charge of Articles of Furniture, vv. 27-32

   f. Merari—in Charge of Boards, Bars, Pillars, Sockets,
and Vessels, vv. 33-37

g. Total of Levites (22,000), vv. 38, 39

h. Census of First-Born of All Israel (22, 273), vv.40-51

4. Service of Levites about the Tabernacle, ch. 4
(Census of Levites [Ages 30-50] for Service)

B. **Cleansing the Camp,** chs. 5-8
(Reason: "Our God is a consuming fire.")

1. Restitution and Jealousy Offering, ch. 5

a. Defilement by Disease and Death, vv. 1-4
For the Christian, lepers represent the flesh;
the dead represent the world.

b. Restitution, vv. 5-10
Repentance is more than saying, "I am sorry"
(2 Cor. 7:10).

c. Jealousy Offering, vv. 11-31
"I am a jealous God."

2. **Vow of the Nazarite;** the Triune Blessing, ch. 6

a. Nazarite Vow, vv. 1-21
Voluntary and temporary

(1) Not to Drink Wine or Strong Drink, v. 3
His joy is to be in the Lord.

(2) Not to Shave Head, v. 5
He is to bear shame (I Cor. 11:14)

(3) Not to Touch Dead Body, v. 7
He is to forsake father and mother.

b. Triune Blessing, vv. 22-27

3. **Gifts of the Princes,** ch. 7
All give the same. The smallest gift is recorded.

4. Light of Lampstand and Laver for Levites, ch. 8

 a. Light of Lampstand, vv. 1-4
 (Walking in the Light)

 b. Levites Cleansed, vv. 5-26
 The Christian's cleansing is by the Word.

II. FORWARD MARCH! chs. 9, 10

A. **Passover** and Covering **Cloud,** ch. 9

 1. Passover Observed by All on Wilderness March, vv. 1-14

 2. Pillar of Cloud by Day, Pillar of Fire by Night, vv. 15-23

B. Silver **Trumpets,** 10:1-10
 (Used for moving Israel on wilderness march, and calling an assembly.)

C. *Forward March!* **Order of March,** 10:11-32
 (See chart.)

D. Halt! vv. 33-36

III. FROM SINAI to Kadesh, chs. 11, 12

A. **Complaining** and Murmuring
 of People Displeasing to the Lord, ch. 11
 Complaining is initiated by the "mixed multitude" (vv. 4-6).
 God provides quail because of dissatisfaction with manna.
 When Moses complains, God permits the appointment of elders.

B. **Jealousy** of Miriam and Aaron; Judgment of Miriam, ch. 12
 (Rebellion in high places, an infection which delays the march.)

IV. FAILURE at Kadesh, chs. 13, 14
(Place of Decision, Great Breach of the Covenant)

A. Spies Chosen and Sent
into Land of Canaan; Return and Report, ch. 13

   1. Cause for Sending Spies (cp. Dt. 1:22), vv. 1-3

   2. Choice of Spies, vv. 4-16

   3. Commission of Spies, vv. 17-20

   4. Conduct of Spies, vv. 21-25
    (Did a thorough job)

   5. Confirmation of Facts, vv. 26, 27

   6. Misinterpretation of Facts, vv. 28, 29; 31-33
    (Majority report: giants vs. grasshoppers)

   7. Right Interpretation of Facts, v. 30
    (Minority report: reliance upon God)

B. Israel Refuses to Enter Because of Unbelief, ch. 14
"So we see that they could not enter in because of unbelief" (Heb. 3:7-19.)

V. FALTERING, FUMBLING and FUSSING through the Wilderness, chs. 15-25

(Silent years—only 4 incidents recorded—no connected history: [1] log, 33:19-37; [2] did not circumcise children, Josh. 5:5,6; [3] did not offer sacrifices to God, Jer. 7:22; Amos 5:25, 26; [4] worshipped idols, Acts 7:42, 43.)

A. Delay God's Blessing; Do Not Destroy God's Purpose, ch. 15

God goes forward; the people go backward. He gives rules for the land. God said they would enter—it was as good as done. 38 years later a new generation of Israel enters the land. These are the children that the fathers thought might perish (14:31).

(Death penalty for breaking sabbath [vv.32-36]. Do all commandments carry death penalty?)

B. Incidents Relating to the Priesthood, chs. 16-19

1. **Gainsaying of Korah,** ch. 16
(5th Murmuring [vv. 1-3])

Rebellion against divinely constituted authority. Korah, a man of great authority, has his place in the camp; Moses has his. Rebellion must be dealt with.

(6th Murmuring [v. 41])

Judgment is stayed by Moses.

2. **Aaron's Rod that Budded,** ch. 17

Office of Aaron is attested by resurrection (v. 8). Christ is priest after order of Melchizedec, established a priest after His resurrection from the dead.

3. Confirmation of Priesthood, ch. 18
(Charge and Position of Aaron and Levites)

Levites receive tithes and give tithes (v. 26)

4. Offering and Ashes of Red Heifer, ch. 19

(Purpose: cleansing the redeemed. Cp. Gal. 6:1)

5. **Deaths** of Miriam and Aaron; **Water from the Rock,** ch. 20

a. At Kadesh Again (After 37 Years), v. 1

b. 7th Murmuring, vv. 2-6

c. Water from Rock; Disobedience of Moses, vv. 7-13

d. Edom Refuses Israel Passage through Their Land, vv. 14-21

e. Death of Aaron, vv. 22-29

6. First Victory of Israel; First Song; **Serpent of Brass,** ch. 21

(8th Murmuring [v. 5]
Serpent of Brass [v. 9, cp. John 3:14],
Israel Sings [v. 17]).

7. The **Prophet Balaam,** chs. 22-25

    a. "The Way of Balaam"—Covetousness
      (cp. 2 Pet. 2:15, 16), ch. 22

    b. "The Error of Balaam"— Ignorance
      of God's Righteousness (cp. Rom. 8:31-34), ch. 23

    c. "The Doctrine of Balaam"—Fornication
      with Moabites; Embrace Their Idolatry, chs. 24, 25

VI. FUTURE (New) Generation Prepare to Enter Land, chs. 26-36

A. Census of New Generation (v. 64), ch. 26

(Less than 1st census (cp. 1:46 with 26:7])

B. Woman's Place Under Law, ch. 27

*Daughters of Zelophehad claim possession of their father.
Moses appeals to God for a decision. God grants their request.*

C. The Law of Offerings, chs. 28, 29

*The offerings illustrate the abiding preciousness of Christ,
what God thinks of Christ. True worship is thinking God's
thoughts after Him.*

D. Law of Vows, ch. 30

*A vow is inviolate.
A woman's vow depends upon her father or husband.
The vow of a widow or divorced woman must stand.*

E. Judgment of Midian, ch. 31
    (Moses' Last Act)

Numbers

    Midian in the wilderness is a type of the world.
The Christian is to be separated from the world
(cp. Gal. 6:14; I John 2:15-17).

F. Reuben and Gad Ask for Land on Wrong Side of Jordan, ch. 32

    Jordan is a type of death and resurrection of Christ

G. Log of the Journeys, ch. 33

H. Borders of Promised Land, ch. 34

 I. Cities of Refuge Given to Levites, ch. 35

    (To be used as refuge for manslayers)

J. Law of Land Regarding Inheritance, ch. 36

    (Land to remain in tribe and family)

RECOMMENDED BOOKS FOR FURTHER STUDY:
(See Genesis)

Boyd, Eleanor H.: *The Gospel in Numbers.*
Erdman, Charles R.: *The Book of Numbers.*
Mackintosh, C. H.: *Notes on Numbers.*

DEUTERONOMY

"The Book of Experience and Obedience"

WRITER: Moses (see Genesis outline)

Moses talked with God face to face. Moses knew God.

The children of Israel saw the acts of God but did not know Him. Moses knew His ways (Psa. 103:7). Deuteronomy is the result of this intimate knowledge plus the experience of 40 years in the wilderness.

Deuteronomy 34:5-12 was probably written by Joshua and belongs to the book of Joshua. When the book of Joshua was written, it was placed on the scroll of the Pentateuch, making a Hexateuch.

TITLE: Deuteronomy

Deuteronomy means "second law." This is not to infer that it is a repetition of the law as given to Moses on Mt. Sinai. It is the law interpreted in the light of 38 years experience in the wilderness. New situations and problems arose which were not covered by the law specifically. There needed to be an application of the law to life situations. (A notable example of this [Num. 27] is the case of the inheritance of the daughters of Zelophehad who had left no sons.)

Deuteronomy, therefore, is more than a mere recapitulation of the law of Sinai, it is another illustration of the law of recurrence (29:1). Specific laws that needed emphasis are repeated and enlarged upon (e.g. the 10 Commandments in chapter 5). Deuteronomy is a commentary on the Mosaic law.

There are 4 Hebrew titles of Deuteronomy:
  (1) Debarim—"The Words" or "These be the Words"
  (2) The Kith of the Fifth of the Law
  (3) The Book of Reproofs
  (4) The Iteration of the Law

KEY: Love and obey

Love *of* God—Deut. 4:37; 7:7-8; 23:5

Deuteronomy

Obey God—Deut. 4:40; 11:26-28; 30:8-20
Love *for* God—6:4, 5; 30:6, 16, 20

This book teaches man to love and to obey God. The word *love* occurs 22 times, *obey* occurs 10 times. The motive for obedience is love. The Lord Jesus says, "If ye love me keep my commandments." The true motive for obedience is stated in Deut. 6:4, 5. God's love for man is the motive for His government and the giving of laws. Man's love of God is the motive for his obedience. This is not the Gospel, but the principle of it is here. This is the pathway of blessing. It is likewise the answer to those who do not find love in the Old Testament. There *is* love in the Old Testament, and there is law in the New Testament. Moses pleads with them to obey.

Why obey? Pleading of Moses:

1. Israel belonged to God (14:1)
2. God loved them (4:37)
3. God wanted to preserve and prosper them (4:1)
4. Their show of gratitude (4:7, 8).

COMMENT:

A new generation had arrived on the east bank of the Jordan River (Deut. 1:5) one month before entering the promised land (Deut. 1:3). Those of the generation which had left Egypt were dead and their bones were bleaching beneath the desert skies because of their unbelief and disobedience.

They had broken God's law—sins of commission;
They had failed to believe God— sins of omission.

The law was "weak through the flesh."

Moses gives to this new generation his final instructions from the Lord before he relinquishes leadership of the nation through death. He reviews the desert experiences, reemphasizes certain features of the law, reveals their future course in light of the Palestinian Covenant, teaches them a new song, blesses the twelve tribes, and then prepares to die. A requiem to Moses concludes the book.

This new generation was unfamiliar with the experiences of Mt. Sinai, and they needed to have the law called to their attention and interpreted in the light of their experience and future dwelling in the promised land.

STRIKING FEATURES:

1. **Greatest doctrinal statement in Old Testament:** Deut. 6:4.

2. **First mention of the Great Tribulation:** Deut. 4:29-31.

3. **Promise of a coming Prophet:** Deut. 18:15-19.

4. **Test for determining true and false prophets:** Deut. 18:20-22.

5. **Prewritten history of Israel in the land before they enter the land:** Deut. 28-30.

6. **Palestinian Covenant:** Deut. 29-30:10.

7. **The Song of Moses—Prophetic:** Deut. 32.

8. **Lonely and strange death of Moses.** (One translation has it, ". . . died by the kiss of God"—God kissed Moses and put him to sleep. What a lovely thought!): Deut. 34:5-8.

OUTLINE:

I. **Reviewing the Journeys, chs. 1-4**

II. **Restating the Law—Love and Obedience, chs. 5-26**

   1. Repetition and Interpretation of 10 Commandments, chs. 5-7

   2. Religious and National Regulations, chs. 8-21
      (1) God's Past Dealings are Assurance for Future, ch. 8
      (2) God Knew Israel—Past Was Not Good, ch. 9
      (3) God Sent Israel to Egypt;
         God Brought Them Out of Egypt, ch. 10
      (4) Promised Land not Like Egypt;
         Principle of Occupancy, ch. 11

Deuteronomy

      (5) Israel Has Only One Place to Worship in Land, ch. 12
      (6) Warning Against and Test
          of False Prophets, False Gods, ch. 13
      (7) Diet for Israel, ch. 14
      (8) God's Poverty Program; the Permanent Slave;
          the Perfect Sacrifice is Christ, ch. 15
      (9) Three Main Feasts—All Males Required to Attend, ch. 16
          (Passover, Pentecost, Tabernacles)
    (10) Sundry Laws, ch. 17
    (11) Priests and Prophets; Test of True Prophet, ch. 18
    (12) Cities of Refuge;
         Extent of Land and Extremity of Law, ch. 19
    (13) Laws Regulating Warfare, ch. 20
    (14) Laws Regulating Murder,
         Marriage and Delinquent Sons, ch. 21

  3. Regulations for Domestic and Personal Relations, chs. 22-26
      (1) Miscellaneous Laws Concerning
          Brother Relationships, Dress,
          Building Code, Planting Seed, and Marriage, ch. 22
      (2) The World, the Flesh and the Devil, ch. 23
      (3) Divorce, ch. 24
      (4) Punishment of Guilty (40 Stripes);
          Law Protecting Widows;
          Punishment for Crimes; Judgment of Amalek, ch. 25
      (5) First Fruits—Thanksgiving, ch. 26

III. Regarding the Future in the Land, chs. 27-30
    (Blessings and Curses)

IV. Requiem to Moses, chs. 31-34

One Hebrew division of Deuteronomy is very good and follows the generally accepted pattern:

EIGHT ORATIONS

1st Oration—1:6-4:40   5th Oration—31:1-13
2nd Oration—4:44-26:19   6th Oration—32 (Song of Moses)
3rd Oration—27-28   7th Oration—33
4th Oration—29-30   8th Oration—34

RECOMMENDED BOOKS:

(See Genesis list.)

Mackintosh, C. H.: *Notes on Deuteronomy*. Loizeaux Brothers, Inc., New York, N.Y.

JOSHUA

WRITER: Joshua (Josh. 24:26). successor to Moses (Deut. 31:23)

The Talmud says that Joshua wrote all but the last 5 verses, and that those were written by Phineas.

Joshua means "Jehovah is Salvation"—the same word in the New Testament is *Jesus* (Heb. 4:8).

Joshua was a great general, born a slave in Egypt.
    40 years old at time of Exodus (one of spies),
    80 years old when he received his commission,
    110 years old at his death.

He was a man of prayer, courage, dependence upon God, faith, leadership, enthusiasm, and fidelity. He is a type of Christ in name and work.

Joshua shows that a man of average ability may become a leader in the church, received his call not in flaming letters across the sky, but from an old man, who knew God and knew Joshua, and saw that he was fitted by God to be a leader.
                                                    —Blackwood

PURPOSE:

Complete redemption out of Egypt. Salvation is not only a redemption from hell, but it is a redemption to heaven.

Who was delivered for our offenses, and was raised again for our justification [Rom. 4:25].

If the second book of the Bible should be called Exodus, then this one should be, to coin a new word, *Eisodus*.

TRANSITION:

Up to this point Jehovah had spoken by dreams, visions, or by angelic ministry. Now a new method is introduced. The law of Moses is the written voice of Jehovah (Josh. 1:8).

34

KEY VERSE: Josh. 1:3.

Joshua compares to Ephesians in the New Testament.
It is prophetic of Israel, and typical of the church.
Read Israel's free title to the land (Jer. 23:8; Ezek. 37:21).
Conflict and conquest go with possession.

KEY WORD: Possession

Israel's ownership was unconditional (Gen. 12:7; 15:18-21; 17:8).

Israel's possession was conditional (Deut. 29:9 - 30:20).

Key word is not "victory"—God gets the victory.
Israel gets deliverance and possession.

Joshua   1:4—Extent of promised land.
13:1—They did not possess it all.
11:16—Joshua had conquered the land and it was available.
11:23—Each tribe was given an allotment, but had to drive out the enemy. There was to be a gradual occupation of the land by each tribe.

The Christian today is given title to spiritual blessings (Eph. 1:3; Rom. 5:1-11; Rom. 8:37; I Cor. 1:30; Gal. 5:22-23).

The practical possession and experience of them depends upon conflict and conquest (Eph. 6:10-20; Gal. 5:25; II Cor. 10:3-6; I Cor. 9:25-27; Heb. 4:11).

These are never attained through the energy of the flesh, but through the power of the Holy Spirit working in the yielded life of the believer (Rom. 7 and 8).

OUTLINE:

I. THE LAND ENTERED. chs. 1-12

1. **Commission** and **Command** of Joshua, ch. 1

2. **Contact** of Spies with Rahab, ch. 2

Joshua

3. **Crossing** the Jordan, ch. 3

4. **Construction** of 2 Memorials, ch. 4

5. **Conditioned** for Conquest, ch. 5

6. **Center** of Land Attacked, chs. 6-8
   (a) Conquest of Jericho, ch. 6
   (b) Conquest of Ai, chs. 7-8

7. **Campaign** in the South, chs. 9, 10
   (a) Compact with the Gibeonites, ch. 9
   (b) Conquer 5 Kings of Amorites, ch. 10
       (Miracle of Sun)

8. **Campaign** in the North, ch. 11
   (Conclusion of Joshua's leadership in War)

9. **Conquered** Kings Listed, ch. 12

II. THE LAND DIVIDED, chs. 13-21

1. **Command** of Joshua is Terminated
   Confirmation of Land to 2½ Tribes, ch. 13

2. **Caleb** Given Hebron, ch. 14

3. **Consignment** of Land to the Tribes of Israel, chs. 15-19

4. **Cities** of Refuge, ch. 20

5. **Cities** for Levites, ch. 21

6. **Command** to 2½ Tribes to Return Home
   Construction of Altar to "See To", ch. 22

III. THE LAST MESSAGE OF JOSHUA, chs. 23, 24

1. **Call** to Leaders of Israel for **Courage** & Certainty, ch. 23

2. **Call** to All Tribes of Israel for **Consecration** and
   Consideration of Covenant with God
   Death of Joshua, ch. 24

RECOMMENDED BOOKS FOR FURTHER STUDY:

Mackintosh, C. H.: *Miscellaneous Writings,* Vol. VI.
Massee, J. C.: *Conflict and Conquest in Holiness.*

JUDGES

A Philosophy of History

Righteousness exalteth a nation: but sin is a reproach to any people [Prov. 14:34].

WRITER: Unknown

This book comes from the period of the monarchy, judging by the phrase which occurs 4 times, "In those days there was no king in Israel" (17:6; 18:1; 19:1; 21:25). Probably written by Samuel.

KEY VERSE: Judges 21:25 (last verse in book)

THEME: Backsliding—and the amazing grace of God in recovering and restoring.

PURPOSE: The book of Judges serves a twofold purpose.

(1) Historically it records the history of the nation from the death of Joshua to Samuel, the last of the judges and the first of the prophets. It bridges the gap between Joshua and the rise of the monarchy. There was no leader to take Joshua's place in the way he had taken Moses' place. This was the trial period of the theocracy after they entered the land.

(2) Morally it was the time of the deep declension of the people as they turned from the unseen leader and descended to the low level of "In those days there was no king in Israel: every man did that which was right in his own eyes." (Compare Judges 1:1 with 20:18.) This should have been an era of glowing progress, but it was a dark day of repeated failure.

This course can be plotted like a hoop rolling down the hill of time. The steps of a nation's downfall are outlined in the last division of the book (see outline). Isaiah, chapter 1, presents these same fatal steps downward that led to final captivity of the nation.

The nation serving God

Delivered

Did evil

Judges raised up

Forsook God

A CYCLE OF HISTORY

Followed own way (pleasure)

Repented

Turned to God

Sold into slavery (depression and war)

Cried to God

Slavery

Servitude

OUTLINE:

I. Introduction to Era of the Judges, chs. 1, 2

1. Condition of Nation After Death of Joshua (Revealed in Limited Victories of Tribes of Judah, Simeon, Benjamin, Manasseh, Ephraim, Zebulun, Asher, Naphtali, Dan), ch. 1

2. God Feeds Into Computer of History Israel's Cycle in Period of the Judges, ch. 2

II. Era of Judges, chs. 3-16

1st Apostasy; Conquered by Mesopotamia; Delivered through Othniel, the Judge, 3:1-11

2nd Apostasy; Conquered by Moabites and Philistines; Delivered Through Ehud and Shamgar, the Judges, 3:12-31

3rd Apostasy; Conquered by Jabin, King of Canaan; Delivered through Deborah and Barak, the Judges, 4:1-5:31

4th Apostasy; Conquered by Midian; Delivered through Gideon, the Judge, 6:1-8:32

5th Apostasy; Civil War; Delivered
through Abimelech, Tola, Jair, the Judges, 8:33-10:5

6th Apostasy; Conquered by Philistines and Ammonites; Delivered through Jephthah, Ibzan, Elon, Abdon, the Judges,
10:6-12:15

7th Apostasy; Conquered by Philistines;
Delivered Partially through Samson, the Judge, chs. 13-16

III. **Results of Era of Judges** (Confusion), **chs. 17-21**

1. Religious Apostasy (The Temple) chs. 17, 18

2. Moral Awfulness (The Home), ch. 19

3. Political Anarchy (The State), chs. 20, 21

RECOMMENDED BOOKS FOR FURTHER STUDY:

Mackintosh, C. H.: *Miscellaneous Writings,* Vol. VI.
Ridout, Samuel: *Overcoming in the Days of Ruin.*

RUTH

An addendum to the book of Judges
A brochure of beauty
A bright picture on the black background of the Judges

WRITER: Samuel could have been the writer.

KEY VERSE: Ruth 3:18

THEME: The Kinsman-redeemer

FEATURES:

(1) A love story without using the word *love*.

(2) The story of a prodigal family who went to the far country.

(3) The only example of the law of the kinsman-redeemer (Hebrew *goel*) in action. Also shows how other laws of the Mosaic system operated.

(4) Furnishes the link between the tribe of Judah and David. The genealogy at the end of the book becomes a most important document. It is found again in the first chapter of Matthew.

(5) A lovely picture of Christ and the Church.

COMMENT:

We prefer not to break up this beautiful love story with notes and outline of extended length. However we refer the reader to our book, *Ruth, Romance of Redemption*, in which we attempt to tell this love story with all of its tenderness, sweetness and loveliness.

OUTLINE:

I.   In the **Land of Moab,** ch. 1

Ruth

II. In the **Field of Boaz,** ch. 2

III. On the **Threshing Floor of Boaz,** ch. 3

IV. In the **Heart and Home of Boaz,** ch. 4

RECOMMENDED BOOKS:

McGee, J. Vernon: *Ruth, Romance of Redemption.*
Moorehouse, Henry: *Ruth, the Moabitess.*

I & II SAMUEL

"I gave thee a king in mine anger, and took him away in my wrath" (Hos. 13:11).

I, II Samuel give us the origin of the kingdom.

The two books of Samuel were classified as one in the Jewish canon.

They are the first two of four books of Kings in the Latin Vulgate.

WRITER:

The name of Samuel is identified with these first two historical books, not because he was the writer primarily, but because his story occurs first and is so prominent. He anointed as king both Saul and David. Samuel is considered the author up to I Samuel 25 (his death). Nathan and Gad completed the writing (I Chron. 29:29, A.S.V.).

FAMILIAR FEATURES:

1. The rise of the kingdom.
2. The story of Hannah.
3. The story of little Samuel.
4. The story of David and Goliath.
5. The friendship of David and Jonathan.
6. King Saul's visit to witch of Endor.
7. God's covenant with David in II Sam. 7.
8. David's great sin—Bathsheba.
9. David's rebellious son—Absalom.

THEME:

Prayer—I Sam. opens with prayer; II Sam. closes with prayer.

Kingdom—the change of the government from a theocracy to a kingdom. God's covenant with David.

Prophet—the rise of the office of prophet, who is now the messenger of God in place of the priest.

KEY VERSE: I Sam. 10:25

COMMENT:

There is a striking contrast between the characters in the book
of Judges and the two books of Samuel. The men in Judges seem
to be ordinary and average while here the characters are outstand-
ing and above the average. There are 6 who stand out in I Samuel.
They are Hannah, Eli, Samuel, Saul, Jonathan and David. I Samuel is a transitional book from the era of the judges to the kingdom. The kingdom foreshadows the coming millennial kingdom
in some respects. There are certain profound global lessons for us
in the setting up of the kingdom. The world needs:

1. A king with power, who exercises his power righteously;
2. A king who will be in full dependence upon God and who can
be trusted with power;
3. A king who is in full obedience to God.

CHAPTERS AND VERSES WORTH REMEMBERING:

I Sam. 15:22—Samuel's word about obedience
I Sam. 25:29—Abigail's word about David's relationship to God
II Sam. 3:33—Abner's epitaph
II Sam. 7— God's covenant with David (N.B. the 7 "I wills")
II Sam. 18:33—David's grief over Absalom
II Sam. 22—Song of David (Psa. 18)
II Sam. 24:24—David's rebuke against a cheap religion

I SAMUEL

OUTLINE:

I. SAMUEL, God's Prophet, chs. 1-8

   1. **Birth** of Samuel
      (1) Hannah's Prayer and Answer, ch. 1
      (2) Hannah's Prophetic Prayer; Boy Samuel in Temple, ch. 2

(3) David Escapes to Nob and Gath, ch. 21
(4) David Gathers His Men; Saul Slays Priests of God, ch. 22
(5) David Fights Philistines; Saul Pursues David;
      Jonathan and David Make Covenant, ch. 23
(6) David Spares Saul's Life at En-gedi, ch. 24
(7) Samuel Dies; David and Abigail, ch. 25
(8) David Again Spares Saul's Life
      in Wilderness of Ziph, ch. 26
(9) David Retreats to Land of Philistia (Ziklag), ch. 27
(10) Saul Goes to Witch of En-dor, ch. 28
(11) Philistines Do Not Trust David in Battle, ch. 29
(12) David Fights Amalekites
      Because of Destruction of Ziklag, ch. 30

4. **Saul,** Mortally **Wounded** in Battle, Commits **Suicide,** ch. 31

RECOMMENDED BOOKS:

(See Genesis list.)

Ridout, Samuel: *King Saul—The Man After the Flesh.*

II SAMUEL

II Samuel continues the message of I Samuel. It is given over entirely to the reign of David. The life and times of David are important because he is the ancestor of Jesus (Matt. 1:1). It shows that government of this world in the hands of man is a failure.

OUTLINE:

I. TRIUMPHS of David, chs. 1-10

1. David Mourns the Death of Saul and Jonathan, ch. 1

2. David Made King over Judah, ch. 2

3. Civil War—Abner Joins with David
   but Murdered by Joab, ch. 3

4. Ish-bosheth, Son of Saul, Killed, ch. 4

5. David Made King Over All Israel;
    Moves His Capital to Jerusalem, ch. 5

6. David's Wrong and Right Attempts
    to Bring Ark to Jerusalem, ch. 6

7. God's Covenant to Build House of David, ch. 7

8. David Consolidates His Kingdom, ch. 8

9. David Befriends Mephibosheth, ch. 9

10. David Wars Against Ammon and Syria, ch. 10

II. TROUBLES of David, chs. 11-24

1. David's Two Great Sins, ch. 11

2. Nathan Faces David with His Sins; David Repents, ch. 12

3. David's Daughter Tamar Raped by Amnon, David's Son;
   Amnon Murdered by Absalom, David's Son, ch. 13

4. David Permits Absalom to Return
   with Half-hearted Forgiveness, ch. 14

5. Absalom Rebels against David, ch. 15

6. Ziba, Mephibosheth's Servant, Deceives David;
   Shimei Curses David, ch. 16

7. Absalom's Advisers (Ahithophel & Hushai)
   Disagree on Attack against David, ch. 17

8. Absalom Slain and David Mourns, ch. 18

9. David Restored to Throne, ch. 19

10. Sheba Revolts against David, ch. 20

II Samuel

RECOMMENDED BOOKS:

(See Genesis list.)

Mackintosh, C. H.: *Miscellaneous Writings,* Vol. I.

I & II KINGS

(The second in the series of 3 double books. Originally one book, they were divided by the Septuagint translators.)

WRITER:

Although the writer is unknown, it was written while the first Temple was still standing (I Kings 8:8). Jeremiah is the traditional writer. Modern scholarship assigns the authorship to "the prophets."

THEME:

Standard of the kingdom: "as David his father" (repeated 9 times in I Kings). It was a human standard but man failed to attain even to it.

KEY VERSES: II Kings 17:22, 23 and 25:21

PROMINENT FEATURES:

1. Practically all the rulers were evil.
2. God's patience in dealing with them.
3. Names of the mothers are given of both good and bad kings.
4. God's grace in sending revival when the king, with the people, turned to Him.
5. Prominence of the prophet and insignificance of the priest.
6. God's long delay before the captivity of both Israel and Judah.
7. Man's total inability to rule for God.
8. Wicked kings who had godly sons, also good kings who had wicked sons.

KINGDOM:

I Kings records the *division* of the kingdom;

II Kings records the *collapse* of the kingdom.

Considered together, they open with King David and close with the King of Babylon.

They are the book of man's rule of God's kingdom.

I & II Kings

The throne on earth must be in tune with the throne in heaven if blessings come and benefits accrue to the people. Yet man's plan cannot overthrow God's purposes.

PURPOSE:

It is a continuation of the narrative begun in I & II Samuel. Actually I & II Samuel with I & II Kings can be viewed as one book. In these books the history of the nation is traced from the time of its greatest extent, influence and prosperity under David and Solomon to the division and finally the captivity and exile of both kingdoms.

The moral teaching is to show man his inability to rule himself and the world. In these four historical books we have the rise and fall of the kingdom of Israel.

OUTLINE:

I. **Death of David,** I Kings **1, 2**

II. **Glory of SOLOMON'S REIGN,** I Kings **3-11**

    1. Solomon's Prayer for Wisdom, chs. 3, 4
    2. Building of Temple, chs. 5-8
    3. Fame of Solomon, chs. 9, 10
    4. Shame and Death of Solomon, ch. 11

III. **DIVISION of the Kingdom,** I Kings **12** - II Kings **16**
    (See chart, next page)

IV. **CAPTIVITY of ISRAEL by Assyria,** II Kings **17**

V. **DECLINE and CAPTIVITY of JUDAH by Babylon,**
                                    II Kings **18-25**

RECOMMENDED BOOKS:

(See Genesis list.)

Eason, J. Lawrence: *New Bible Survey*
Mackintosh, C. H.: *Miscellaneous Writings.*

CHRONOLOGICAL TABLE OF THE KINGS OF THE DIVIDED KINGDOM

J U D A H

King	Reign	Character	Prophet
1. Rehoboam	931-913 B.C. (17 yrs.)	Bad	Shemaiah
2. Abijah	913-911 (3 yrs.)	Bad	
3. Asa	911-870 (41 yrs.)	Good	
4. Jehoshaphat	870-848* (25 yrs.)	Good	
5. Jehoram	848-841* (8 yrs.)	Bad	
6. Ahaziah	841 (1 yr.)	Bad	
7. Athaliah	841-835 (6 yrs.)	Bad	
8. Joash	835-796 (40 yrs.)	Good	Joel
9. Amaziah	796-767 (29 yrs.)	Good	
10. Azariah (or Uzziah)	767-740* (52 yrs.)	Good	Isaiah
11. Jotham	740-732* (16 yrs.)	Good	Micah
12. Ahaz	732-716 (16 yrs.)	Bad	
13. Hezekiah	716-687 (29 yrs.)	Good	
14. Manasseh	687-642* (55 yrs.)	Bad	Nahum
15. Amon	642-640 (2 yrs.)	Bad	{ Habakkuk / Zephaniah
16. Josiah	640-608 (31 yrs.)	Good	Jeremiah
17. Jehoahaz	608 (3 mo.)	Bad	
18. Jehoiakim	608-597 (11 yrs.)	Bad	
19. Jehoiachin	597 (3 mo.)	Bad	
20. Zedekiah	597-583 (11 yrs.)	Bad	

(Destruction of Jerusalem and captivity of Judah)

*Co-regency

I S R A E L

King	Reign	Character	Prophet
1. Jeroboam I	931-910 B.C. (22 yrs.)	Bad	Ahijah
2. Nadab	910-909 (2 yrs.)	Bad	
3. Baasha	909-886 (24 yrs.)	Bad	
4. Elah	886-885 (2 yrs.)	Bad	
5. Zimri	885 (7 days)	Bad	
6. Omri	885-874* (12 yrs.)	Bad	{ Elijah
7. Ahab	874-853 (22 yrs.)	Bad	Micaiah
8. Ahaziah	853-852 (2 yrs.)	Bad	
9. Joram	852-841 (12 yrs.)	Bad	Elisha
10. Jehu	841-814 (28 yrs.)	Bad	
11. Jehoahaz	814-798 (17 yrs.)	Bad	
12. Jehoash	798-782 (16 yrs.)	Bad	
13. Jeroboam II	782-753* (41 yrs.)	Bad	{ Jonah / Amos / Hosea
14. Zechariah	753-752 (6 mo.)	Bad	
15. Shallum	752 (1 mo.)	Bad	
16. Menahem	752-742 (10 yrs.)	Bad	
17. Pekahiah	742-740 (2 yrs.)	Bad	
18. Pekah	740-732* (20 yrs.)	Bad	
19. Hoshea	732-721 (9 yrs.)	Bad	

(Capture of Samaria and captivity of Israel)

*Co-regency

I & II CHRONICLES

The ACTS of the Old Testament

WRITER: Probably Ezra. There is a striking resemblance in style and language to the books of Ezra and Nehemiah. Evidently Chronicles was written during the Babylonian Captivity. It could have been a compilation of diaries and journals of the priests and prophets, assembled by Ezra. These two books of Chronicles not only constituted one book in the original, but apparently also included Ezra and Nehemiah. This lends support to the authorship of Ezra and supports the Jewish tradition. Scholars have noted a similarity in the Hebrew of all four books.

COMMENT:

Many treat Chronicles and Kings as if they were "Cabbages and Kings." Are the Chronicles a duplication of Kings? Although they cover the same ground from Saul to Zedekiah, they are not duplications. Greek translators gave Chronicles the title of "Things Omitted"—there is more here which does not occur in the other historical books. This is another instance of the law of recurrence or recapitulation, seen previously in Genesis 2 and Deuteronomy, by which God goes over ground which had already been covered in order to add details and to emphasize that which He considers important. This is exactly the case in Chronicles. David is the subject of I Chronicles; the house of David is prominent in II Chronicles. Chronicles gives the history of Judah while practically ignoring the Northern Kingdom. Chronicles does not record David's sin—when God forgives, He forgets. The Temple and Jerusalem are prominent in Chronicles. In Kings the history of the nation is given from the throne; in Chronicles it is given from the altar. In Kings the palace is the center; in Chronicles the Temple is the center. Kings records the political history; Chronicles records the religious history. Chronicles is an interpretation of Kings—hence the constant reference in Kings to Chronicles. Kings gives us man's viewpoint. Chronicles gives us God's viewpoint (note this well as you read Chronicles and it will surprise you).

I CHRONICLES

OUTLINE:

I. Genealogies, chs. 1-9

This is important to God. We must be sons of God before we can do the work of God. "Ye must be born again" (John 3:7). These help explain the two genealogies of Christ in Matthew and Luke (cf. I Chron. 3:5 with Luke 3:31).

II. Saul's Reign, ch. 10

III. David's Reign, chs. 11-29

1. David's Mighty Men, chs. 11, 12
2. David and the Ark, chs. 13-16
3. David and the Temple, ch. 17
4. David's Wars, chs. 18-20
5. David's Sin in Numbering the People, ch. 21
6. David's Preparation
   and Organization for Building Temple, chs. 22-29

II CHRONICLES

II Chronicles obviously carried on the account begun in I Chronicles with the same point of reference and emphasis. It covers chronologically the same period as Kings with certain notable emphases. The first 9 chapters are given over to the reign of Solomon. Chapter 10 records the division of the kingdom but thereafter only the account of the Southern Kingdom of Judah is given. The spotlight is on the kings who followed in the line of David. Given special prominence are the reigns of 5 of these kings in whose reigns were periods of revival, renewal and reformation.
The kings were:
1. Asa
2. Jehoshaphat
3. Joash
4. Hezekiah
5. Josiah

II Chronicles

II Chronicles concludes with the decree of Cyrus after the 70 years captivity, with no record of the captivity itself. This was "time out" in God's program.

OUTLINE:

I. Solomon's Reign, chs. 1-9
Building the Temple is his most important accomplishment.

II. Division of the Kingdom and History of Judah, chs. 10-36
Reformations Given Prominence:
1. Asa's, chs. 14-16
2. Jehoshaphat's, chs. 17-20
3. Joash's, chs. 23, 24
4. Hezekiah's, chs. 29-32
5. Josiah's, chs. 34, 35

RECOMMENDED BOOKS:

(See Genesis list.)

Mackintosh, C. H.: *Miscellaneous Writings.*

The post-captivity books record the return and restoration at Jerusalem after the 70 years Babylonian captivity as predicted by Jeremiah. 6 books belong to this series. They are divided into 2 groups:

      Historical—Ezra, Nehemiah and Esther;
      Prophetical—Haggai, Zechariah and Malachi.

Although Ezra is a continuation of the historical books begun with Joshua, the pre-captivity and captivity books could be profitably studied before beginning with Ezra. These books include all of the major prophets and the minor prophets, with the exception of the last 3 books of the Old Testament. However, we shall proceed according to the arrangement of the canon of Scripture.

EZRA

WRITER: Ezra

He is one of the characters who has not received proper recognition. He was a descendant of Hilkiah, the high priest (Ezra 7:1) who found a copy of the law during the reign of Josiah (II Chron. 34:14). Ezra, as a priest, was unable to serve during the captivity, but he gave his time to a study of the Word of God—he was "a ready scribe in the law of Moses" (Ezra 7:6). Ezra was a great revivalist and reformer. The revival began with the reading of the Word of God by Ezra (Neh. 8). Also he probably was the writer of I and II Chronicles and of Psalm 119 which exalts the Word of God. He organized the synagogue, was the founder of the order of scribes, helped settle the canon of Scripture and arranged the Psalms.

> *Let us pay tribute to Ezra who was the first to begin a revival of Bible study.*
> *Is this not God's program for revival?*

THEME:

The Word of the Lord. There are 10 direct references—1:1; 3:2; 6:14; 6:18; 7:6, 10, 14; 9:4; 10:3, 5.

Ezra

The place of the Word of God in the total life of His people—religious, social, business and political.

KEY: "Trembled at the words of the God of Israel" (Ezra 9:4; 10:3).

"We already have seen that the Babylonian captivity did not bring the Jews to national repentance, and so lead to national restoration. As the reading of Ezra will disclose, when Cyrus, king of Persia, gave permission to the captives to return to Jerusalem and rebuild the Temple, scarcely 50,000 availed themselves of the privilege, a considerable portion of whom were priests and Levites of the humbler and poorer class."

—Dr. James M. Gray.

OUTLINE:

I. RETURN from BABYLON Led by ZERUBBABEL, chs. 1-6
(About 50,000 returned)

1. **Restoration** of Temple by Decree of Cyrus, ch. 1
2. **Return** under Zerubbabel, ch. 2
3. **Rebuilding** of Temple, ch. 3
4. **Retardation** of Rebuilding by Opposition, ch. 4
   (Decree of Artaxerxes)
5. **Renewal** of Rebuilding of Temple, chs. 5, 6
   (Decree of Darius)

II. RETURN from BABYLON Led by EZRA, chs. 7-10
(About 2,000 returned.)

1. **Return** under Ezra, chs. 7, 8
2. **Reformation** under Ezra, chs. 9, 10

The books of Haggai and Zechariah (Ezra 5:1) should be read and studied with the book of Ezra, for all 3 were written in the shadow of the rebuilt Temple, and were given to encourage the people in building.

RECOMMENDED BOOKS:
(See Genesis list.)

Ironside, H. A.: *Notes on the Book of Ezra.*

NEHEMIAH

(Ezra and Nehemiah are one book in the Hebrew canon.)

WRITER: Perhaps Ezra.

Nehemiah was a layman; Ezra was a priest. In the book of Ezra the emphasis is upon the rebuilding of the Temple; in the book of Nehemiah the emphasis is upon the rebuilding of the walls of Jerusalem. In Ezra we have the religious aspect of the return; in Nehemiah we have the political aspect of the return. Ezra is a fine representative of the priest and scribe; Nehemiah is a noble representative of the business man. Nehemiah had an important office at the court of the powerful Persian king, Artaxerxes, but his heart was with God's people and God's program in Jerusalem. The personal note is the main characteristic of the book.

TIME:

Chronologically, this is the last of the historical books. We have come to the end of the line as far as time is concerned. The Old Testament goes no further. The book of Ezra picks up the thread of the story about 70 years after II Chronicles. The 70 years captivity is over and a remnant returns to the land of Israel. The return under Ezra took place about 50 years after Zerubbabel. Nehemiah returns about 15 years after Ezra. These figures are approximate and are given to show the stages in the history of Israel after the captivity. This enables one to see how the "70 weeks" of Daniel begin with the book of Nehemiah (not with Ezra) "from the going forth of the commandment to restore and build Jerusalem unto the Messiah, the Prince, shall be seven weeks, and threescore and two weeks...." The background of the events of Nehemiah is "...the street shall be built again, and the wall, even in troublous times" (Daniel 9:25).

N.B. The following dates, suggested by Sir Robert Anderson, seem to be a satisfactory solution to the problem of the "70 weeks" of Daniel:

Decree of Cyrus, 536 B.C.—Ezra 1:1-4.
Decree of Artaxerxes, 445 B.C. (20th year of his reign)—Neh. 2:1-8.

"70 weeks" begin.

The 1st "7 weeks" end, 397 B.C. —Malachi.
(For details see Sir Robert Anderson's, *The Coming Prince.*)

KEY WORD:

"So" occurs 32 times. It denotes a man of action and few words. Mark this word in your Bible and notice how this ordinarily unimportant word stands out in this book.

KEY VERSES: Neh. 1:4 and 6:3

OUTLINE:

I. REBUILDING the WALLS, chs. 1-7

1. Nehemiah's **Prayer** for the Remnant at Jerusalem, ch. 1
2. Nehemiah's **Request** of the King; **Return** to Jerusalem; **Review** of the Ruins of Jerusalem, ch. 2:1-16
3. Nehemiah's **Encouragement** to Rebuild the Walls, ch. 2:17-20
4. **Rebuilding** the Walls and the Gates, ch. 3
5. Nehemiah's **Response** to Opposition, chs. 4-6
   (Wall Completed, 6:16)
6. Nehemiah's **Register** of People, ch. 7
   (Only 42,360 people, 7,337 servants and 245 singers returned. Compare this with the fact that Judah alone had 470,000 warriors [I Chron. 21:5].)

II. REVIVAL and REFORM, chs. 8-13

1. Great Bible **Reading** Led by Ezra, ch. 8
2. **Revival** —the Result, chs. 9-10
3. **Reform** —Another Result, chs. 11-13

THE BABYLONIAN CAPTIVITY:

God's chosen people were called to witness against idolatry, but too often they themselves succumbed and became idolators. God sent them to Babylon, the fountainhead of idolatry, to take the gold cure. They returned repudiating idolatry.

Their restoration was incomplete. They were not free from this time on to the time of the Roman Empire. The New Testament opens with them under the rule of Rome.

RECOMMENDED BOOKS:

(See Genesis list.)

Ironside, H. A.: *Notes on the Book of Nehemiah.*

ESTHER

This is one of the two books of the Old Testament named for a woman. While Ruth is the story of a Gentile who married a Jew, Esther is the story of a Jewess who married a Gentile.

WRITER: Unknown

Could Mordecai have been the writer? See Esther 9:29.

KEY VERSE: 4:14

A STRANGE STORY:

God's name is not mentioned in this book; no divine title or pronoun refers to Him. The heathen king's name is mentioned 192 times. (It is true also that God's name does not occur in the Song of Solomon, but every pronoun—with a possible exception of 8:6 —refers to Him.) Esther is the record of Israel in a self-chosen pathway. Opportunity had been given for the Jews to return under Cyrus, but only a very small remnant had returned. Ezra and Nehemiah give the story of those who did return. Esther gives the story of those who did not return, but who rather chose the prosperity and luxury of Persia. They are out of the will of God, but they are not beyond His care. Deuteronomy 31:18 explains the reason God's name does not appear. In the book of Esther His face is hidden. There is no mention of prayer nor dependence upon God in this book. Esther is never quoted in the New Testament, nor is there even a casual reference to it. However the Jews give it a peculiar emphasis. It is one of the 5 books called Megilloth (rolls) and is placed beside the Pentateuch in importance.

MESSAGE OF THE BOOK:

Esther teaches the providence of God. *Providence* comes from the same stem as *provide,* and it means simply that God will provide.

Theologically, providence is the direction God gives to everything, animate and inanimate, good and evil.

Practically, providence is the hand of God in the glove of history—and that glove will never move until He moves it. God is at the steering wheel of this universe. Providence means that God is behind the scenes, shifting and directing them. Providence is the way God coaches the man on second base. It is the way God leads the man who will not be led. As recorded in the book of Esther, the entire Jewish nation would have been slain had it not been for the providence of God. God stands in the shadows, keeping watch over His own.

ANTI-SEMITISM:

This book teaches how God met another satanic attempt to destroy the nation Israel, and how vengeance was wrought upon the perpetrators of the dastardly deed. (See Gen. 12:3.)

OUTLINE:

1. The **Wife** Who **Refused to Obey** Her Husband, ch. 1
2. The **Beauty Contest** to Choose a Real Queen, ch. 2
3. Haman and **Anti-Semitism,** ch. 3
4. **For Such a Time as This,** ch. 4
5. The **Scepter of Grace** and the Nobility of Esther, ch. 5
6. When a **King Could Not Sleep** at Night, ch. 6
7. The **Man Who Came to Dinner** but Died on the Gallows, ch. 7
8. The **Message of Hope** that Went Out from the King, ch. 8
9. The Institution of the **Feast of Purim,** chs. 9-10

RECOMMENDED BOOKS:

(See Genesis list.)

Ironside, H. A.: *Notes on the Book of Esther.*
McGee, J. Vernon: *Esther, Romance of Providence.*

Job is the first of the poetical books, which also include Psalms, Proverbs, Ecclesiastes, Song of Solomon, and Lamentations. The reference is to the form of the content and does not imply imaginative or capricious content. Neither does the term *poetical* mean that it is rhythmic. Hebrew poetry is achieved by repeating an idea, which is called parallelism.

The dialogue in the book of Job is poetry. Conversation was in poetry of that day. The *Iliad* and *Odyssey* of Homer are examples in secular literature.

JOB

WRITER: Unknown

The following have been suggested: Moses, Ezra, Solomon, Job, and Elihu. That Elihu is the writer seems most likely (32:16).

DATE: Unknown

Evidently it was written during the patriarchal period. Did Job know Jacob? It is possible. It was written before Exodus, it would seem, as there is no reference to the Mosaic law, nor to any of the events recorded in the book of Exodus. Here are the arguments which seem to place Job with the patriarchs:

1. Length of Job's life span (Job 42:16).
2. Job acted as high priest in his family.
3. Eliphaz was descended from Esau's eldest son (Gen. 36:10).

PURPOSE: Many problems are raised and settled by this book.

1. To determine why the righteous suffer. (This is not the primary teaching.)
2. To refute the slander of Satan.
3. To reveal Job to himself.
4. To teach patience. Was Job patient?
5. *Primary purpose:* to teach *repentance.*

God selected the best man who ever lived (Christ is the exception) and showed that he needed to repent. In contrast, men choose the worst man who repents as an illustration. Manasseh, a most ungodly king, repented; Saul of Tarsus repented; St. Francis of Assisi, a debauched nobleman, repented; and Jerry MacAuley, a drunken bum, repented. God chose the best man and showed that he repented—"I have heard of thee by the hearing of the ear, but now mine eye seeth thee. Wherefore I abhor myself, and repent in dust and ashes" (Job 42:5, 6).

ESTIMATION:

Tennyson said of the book of Job, "The greatest poem, whether of ancient or modern literature." Carlyle said, "I call that [Job] one of the grandest ever written with pen." Luther said, "More magnificent and sublime than any other book of Scripture." Moorehead said, "The book of Job is one of the noblest poems in existence." *Amen to that*

OUTLINE:

I. DRAMA (Prose), **chs. 1-2:10**

    1. Scene I. Land of Uz. Job's Prosperity & Serenity, 1:1-5
    2. Scene II. Heaven. Satan's Slander of God & Job, 1:6-12
    3. Scene III. Land of Uz.
       Job's Loss of Children & Wealth, 1:13-22
    4. Scene IV. Heaven. God & Satan, 2:1-6
    5. Scene V. Land of Uz.
       Job's Loss of Health & Wife's Sympathy, 2:7-10

II. DIALOGUE (Poetry), **chs. 2:11-42:6**

    1. Scene VI. City Dump, 2:11-37:24
       (1) Job's Loss of Understanding of Friends, 2:11-13
       (2) Job vs. Eliphaz, Bildad, Zophar, 3:1-32:1
       (3) Job vs. Elihu, 32:2-37:24
    2. Scene VII. Jehovah vs. Job, 38:1-42:6

III. EPILOGUE (Prose), **ch. 42:7-17**

Scene VIII. Land of Uz, Job's Blessings Doubled

RECOMMENDED BOOKS:

(See Genesis list.)

Mackintosh, C. H.: *Job and His Friends.*
Reid, R. J.: *How Job Learned His Lesson.*

PSALMS

The Book of Worship
The Hymn Book of the Temple

TITLE:

The title in the Hebrew means *Praises* or *Book of Praises*. The title in the Greek suggests the idea of an instrumental accompaniment. Our title comes from the Greek *psalmos*.

WRITERS:

Many writers contributed one or more Psalms.

David, "the sweet psalmist of Israel," has 73 Psalms assigned to him (Psalm 2 is ascribed to him in Acts 4:25; Psalm 95 in Hebrews 4:7). Also he could be the author of some of the "Orphanic" Psalms. He was peculiarly endowed to write these songs from experience as well as a special aptitude. He arranged those in existence in his day for temple use. The writers are as follows: David 73, Moses 1 (90th), Solomon 2, Sons of Korah 11, Asaph 12, Heman 1 (88th), Ethan 1, (89th), Hezekiah 10, "Orphanic" 39 (David may be the writer of some of these).

THEME:

Christ (the Messiah) is prominent throughout (Luke 24:44). The King and the kingdom are the theme songs of the Psalms.

KEY WORD: Hallelujah

KEY PSALM: Psalm 150

Hallelujah occurs 13 times in 6 verses.

FEATURES:

The Psalms record deep devotion, intense feeling, exalted emotion, and dark dejection. The Psalms play upon the keyboard of the human soul with all the stops pulled out.

They run the psychological gamut. This book has been called the epitomy and anatomy of the soul; also designated as the garden of the Scriptures. The place Psalms have held in the lives of God's people testifies to their universality, although they have a peculiar Jewish application. They express the deep feelings of all believing hearts in all generations.

The Psalms are full of Christ. There is a more complete picture of Him in Psalms than in the Gospels. The Gospels tell us that He went to the mountain to pray, but the Psalms give us His prayer. The Gospels tell us that He was crucified, but the Psalms tell us what went on in His own heart during the crucifixion. The Gospels tell He went back to heaven, but the Psalms begin where the Gospels leave off and show us Christ seated in heaven.

There are many types of Psalms. Although all of them have Christ as the object of worship, some are technically called Messianic Psalms. These record the birth, life, death, resurrection, glory, priesthood, kingship, and return of Christ. The Imprecatory Psalms have caused the most criticism because of their vindictiveness and prayers for judgment. These Psalms came from a time of war and from a people who under law were looking for justice and peace on the earth. (The Christian is told to love his enemies.) They look to a time coming on the earth when the Antichrist will be in power. We have no reasonable basis to say how people should act and what they should say under these circumstances. Other types of Psalms include penitential, historic, pilgrim, Hallel, missionary, puritan, acrostic, and praise of God's Word.

OUTLINE:
(Corresponds to Pentatuech of Moses)

I. Genesis Section, Psalms 1-41

Man seen in a state of blessedness, fall, and recovery
   (Man in View)

Psalm 1—Perfect Man (Last Adam)
Psalm 2—Rebellious Man
Psalm 3—Perfect Man Rejected
Psalm 4—Conflict Between Seed of Woman and Serpent

Psalm 5—Perfect Man in Midst of Enemies
Psalm 6—Perfect Man in Midst of Chastisement (Bruising Heel)
Psalm 7—Perfect Man in Midst of False Witnesses
Psalm 8—Repair of Man Comes Through Man (Bruising Head)
Psalms 9-15—Enemy and Antichrist Conflict; Final Deliverance
Psalms 16-41—Christ in Midst of His People Sanctifying Them to God

II. Exodus Section, Psalms 42-72

Ruin and Redemption (Israel in View)

Psalms 42-49—Israel's Ruin
Psalms 50-60—Israel's Redeemer
Psalms 61-72—Israel's Redemption

III. Leviticus Section, Psalms 73-89

Darkness and Dawn (Sanctuary in View)

Tabernacle, Temple, House, Assembly and Congregation in almost every Psalm.

IV. Numbers Section, Psalms 90-106

Peril and Protection (Earth in View)

V. Deuteronomy Section, Psalms 107-150

Perfection and Praise of the Word of God

Psalm 119, an acrostic in the heart of this section, refers to the Word of God in almost every verse. It is the longest chapter in the Bible.

RECOMMENDED BOOKS:

Alexander, J. A.: *The Psalms Translated and Explained.*
Gaebelein, A. E.: *The Book of Psalms.*
Pettingill, William L.: *Christ in the Psalms.*
Spurgeon, C. H.: *The Treasury of David.*

PROVERBS

WRITER: Solomon

Solomon is the writer of the next 3 books of the Bible: Proverbs, Ecclesiastes, Song of Solomon. Proverbs is the book on wisdom, Ecclesiastes is the book on folly, Song of Solomon is the book on love. Love is the happy medium between wisdom and folly. Solomon is an authority on all 3 subjects (1 Kings 4:32-34).

DEFINITIONS:

"A proverb is a saying that conveys a specific truth in a pointed, pithy way." "Proverbs are short sentences, drawn from long experience." A truth couched in a form that is easy to remember, a philosophy based on experience, and a rule for conduct. A proverb is a sententious sentence, a maxim, an old saying, an old saw, a bromide, and an epigram.

KEY VERSE: Prov. 1:7

FEATURES:

The Orient and Ancient East are the home of proverbs. Evidently Solomon gathered together many from other sources. He was the editor of all, and the author of some. Dr. Thirtle and other scholars noted that there is a change of pronoun in the book from the second person to the third person. Their conclusions are that the proverbs with the third person were by Solomon.

There is a difference between the book of Proverbs and proverbs in other writings (the Greeks were great at making proverbs, especially the gnostic poets):

(1) Proverbs bear no unscientific statement nor inaccurate observation, e.g. "Out of the heart proceed the issues of life" (Prov. 4:23). About 2700 years later Harvey found that the blood circulates. In contrast, in an apocryphal book, the Epistle of Barnabas, mention is made of the mythical phoenix, a bird that consumes itself by fire and rises in resurrection. A fable such as this does not appear in the book of Proverbs, nor anywhere in the Bible.

68

(2) The Proverbs are on a high moral plane. The immoral sayings which occur in other writings are not present. Justyn Martyr said that Socrates was a Christian before Christ. Although he portrays a high conception of morals, according to his admirers, Socrates also gives instructions to harlots on how to conduct themselves. The best that can be said of him is that he is unmoral.

(3) The Proverbs do not contradict, while man's proverbs are often in opposition to each other, e.g. "Look before you leap" vs. "He who hesitates is lost." "A man gets no more than he pays for" vs. "The best things in life are free." "Leave well enough alone" vs. "Progress never stands still." "A rolling stone gathers no moss" vs. "A setting hen does not get fat."

Although the book of Proverbs seems to be a collection of sayings without any particular regard for orderly arrangement, the contrary is true. *The book tells a story. It is a picture of a young man starting out in life. His first lesson is given in 1:7. Two schools bid for him and both send their literature. One is the school of Wisdom, the other is the school for fools.* In chapter 8 the young man goes to the academy of Wisdom where he is taught in proverbs. From chapters 10 through 24 the young man is in the classroom of Wisdom. This book is especially helpful to young men. (A very prominent jeweler in Dallas, Texas, had the book of Proverbs bound attractively and copies given by the hundreds to young men.) The advice herein transcends all dispensations. The One who is *Wisdom is none other than the Lord Jesus Christ* (1 Cor. 1:30). The book of Proverbs is not a hodgepodge of unrelated statements, nor is it a discourse of cabbages and kings (Eccl. 12:9).

There is a proverb that is a *thumbnail* sketch of every character in the Bible (we can suggest only a few). Likewise there is a proverb that will fit *all your friends and acquaintances,* which adds interest to the reading of the book (but may not increase your popularity if you identify them publicly).

Solomon wrote 3000 proverbs (1 Ki. 4:32). We have less than 1000 in this book.

STRUCTURE OF PROVERBS (by A. C. Gaebelein):

The literary form of these Proverbs is mostly in the form of

Proverbs

couplets. The two clauses of the couplet are generally related to each other by what has been termed parallelism, according to Hebrew poetry. Three kinds of of parallelism have been pointed out:

1. *Synonymous Parallelism.* Here the second clause restates what is given in the first clause.

   "Judgments are prepared for scorners,
   And stripes for the back of fools" (Prov. 19:29).

2. *Antithetic (Contrast) Parallelism.* Here a truth, which is stated in the first clause, is made stronger in the second clause by contrast with an opposite truth.

   "The light of the righteous rejoiceth,
   But the lamp of the wicked shall be put out" (Prov. 13:9).

3. *Synthetic Parallelism.* The second clause develops the thought of the first.

   "The terror of a king is as the roaring of a lion;
   He that provoketh him to anger sinneth against his own life" (Prov. 20:2).

OUTLINE:

   I.   **Wisdom** and **Folly** Contrasted, chs. 1-9
   II. Proverbs of **Solomon,** Written and Set in Order by Himself, chs. 10-24
   III. Proverbs of **Solomon,** Set in Order by Men of Hezekiah, chs. 25-29
   IV. Oracle of **Agur,** Unknown Sage, ch. 30
   V.   Proverbs of a **Mother to Lemuel,** ch. 31

RECOMMENDED BOOKS:

(See Genesis list.)

Ironside, H. A.: *Notes on the Book of Proverbs.*

70

ECCLESIASTES

WRITER: Solomon

The book is the "dramatic autobiography of his life when he got away from God."

TITLE: *Ecclesiastes* means "preacher" or "philosopher."

PURPOSE:

The purpose of any book of the Bible is important to the correct understanding of it; this is no more evident than here. Human philosophy, apart from God, must inevitably reach the conclusions in this book; therefore, there are many statements which seem to contradict the remainder of Scripture. It almost frightens us to know that this book has been the favorite of atheists, and they (e.g. Volnay and Voltaire) have quoted from it profusely. Man has tried to be happy without God, and this book shows the absurdity of the attempt. Solomon, the wisest of men, tried every field of endeavor and pleasure known to man; his conclusion was, "All is vanity."

God showed Job, a righteous man, that he was a sinner in God's sight. In Ecclesiastes God showed Solomon, the wisest man, that he is a fool in God's sight.

ESTIMATIONS:

In Ecclesiastes we learn that without Christ we cannot be satisfied, even if we possess the whole world—the heart is too large for the object. In the Song of Solomon we learn that if we turn from the world and set our affections on Christ, we cannot fathom the infinite heart preciousness of His love—the Object is too large for the heart.

Dr. A. T. Pierson says, "There is a danger in pressing the words in the Bible into a positive announcement of scientific fact, so marvelous are some of these correspondencies. But it is certainly a curious fact that Solomon should use language entirely consistent with discoveries as evaporation and storm currents (1:6, 7). Some have boldly said that Redfield's theory of storms is here explicitly stated. Without taking such ground, we ask, who taught Solomon to use terms that readily accommodate facts? Who taught him that the movement of the winds which seem to be so lawless and uncertain, are ruled by laws as positive as those which rule the growth of the plant; and that by evaporation, the waters that fall on the earth are continually rising again, so that the sea never overflows? Ecclesiastes 12:6 is a poetic description of death. The 'silver cord' describes the spinal marrow, the 'golden bowl' the basin which holds the brain, the 'pitcher' the lungs, and the 'wheel' the heart. Without claiming that Solomon was inspired to foretell the circulation of the blood, 26 centuries before Harvey announced it, is it not remarkable that the language he uses exactly suits the facts—a wheel pumping up through one pipe to discharge through another?"

KEY:

"Vanity" occurs 37 times. Most Bible teachers give "under the sun," which occurs 29 times.

OUTLINE:

I. Problem Stated: "All is Vanity," 1:1-3

II. Experiment Made, 1:4-12:12

Seeking Satisfaction in the Following:

1. Science, 1:4-11
2. Wisdom and Philosophy, 1:12-18
3. Pleasure, 2:1-11
4. Materialism (Living for the "Now"), 2:12-26
5. Fatalism, 3:1-15
6. Egoism, 3:16-4:16
7. Religion, 5:1-8
8. Wealth, 5:9-6:12
9. Morality, 7:1-12:12

III. Result of Experiment, 12:13, 14

All things under the sun are vanity.

A right relationship with God, in any age, through the way He has made, brings the only abiding satisfaction.

What a difference between the man "under the sun" and the man "in Christ" seated in the heavenlies far above all suns!

RECOMMENDED BOOKS:

(See Genesis)

Jennings, F. C.: *Old Groans and New Songs.*

SONG OF SOLOMON

WRITER: Solomon (1:1)

Solomon was the author of 1,005 songs (1 Ki. 4:32), but we have only one (Song of Songs). As the name would indicate, it is the best.

KEY WORDS: "Beloved," the name for Him, and "love" the name for her.

KEY VERSES: 6:3 and 8:7

THE MEANING:

The Song of Solomon is a parabolic poem. The *interpretation*, not the inspiration, causes the difficulty—although there are some who actually feel it should not be in the Bible. Since it is in the canon of Scripture, it is the great neglected book of the Bible. Often young preachers are counseled not to use it until they become old men. The Jews called it the Holy of Holies of Scripture. Origen and Jerome tell us that the Jews would not permit their young men to read it until they were thirty years old. Surely any fragile flower requires delicate handling. There have been 4 different and important meanings found in this book:

1. It sets forth the "glory of wedded love"; declaring the sacredness of marital relationship, and that marriage is a divine institution. To our occidental minds it borders on the vulgar, but when it is compared to other oriental poetry, it is indeed tame, and lacks the splash of color and extravagant terms which characterizes oriental poetry (e.g. Persian poetry). The Jews taught that it sets forth the heart of a satisfied husband and a devoted wife.

2. It sets forth the love of Jehovah for Israel. The prophets spoke of Israel as the wife of Jehovah.

These two interpretations have been set forth by the scribes and rabbis of Israel, and have been accepted by the church. However, there are two other interpretations.

3. It is a picture of Christ and the Church. The Church is the bride of Christ, a familiar figure of Scripture (2 Cor. 11:2; Eph. 5:27; Rev. 21).

4. It depicts the communion of Christ and the individual believer. The soul's communion with Christ is here set forth.

"The Song of Solomon tests the spiritual capacity of the reader."

STORY OUTLINE:

Since this book is a series of scenes, in a drama that is not told in chronological sequence, we shall make no attempt to outline the book.

The popular interpretation, that it tells the story of a girl kidnapped by Solomon, is repugnant. The book of Dr. H. A. Ironside is especially recommended, as it contains the only adequate and satisfying interpretation that I have seen. The key to the story is found in 8:11. The story is of a poor family of Ephraim in which there is a girl who is a sort of Cinderella. The poverty of the family forces her into the vineyards where she meets the young shepherd. The story of their love is first told. Then he leaves her with the promise that he will return. He is absent for a long time, and she despairs of his return. One day the electrifying word is shouted along the way that King Solomon is coming by. She is not interested, and takes no further notice until word is brought her that King Solomon wants to see her. She is puzzled until she is brought into his presence where she recognizes him as her shepherd lover. He takes her to his palace in Jerusalem where most of the song takes place.

COMMENT:

The setting of the drama is the palace in Jerusalem, and some of the scenes are flash-backs to a previous time. There is a reminder here of the Greek drama where a chorus talks back and forth to the protagonists of the play. The daughters of Jerusalem carry along the tempo of the story. Some of these dialogues were evidently to be sung. Several lovely scenes are introduced at Jerusalem which find a counterpart in the Church.

Song of Solomon

When reading the Song of Solomon, take off the shoes from the natural man, for the ground on which you stand is spiritual ground.

RECOMMENDED BOOKS:

(See Genesis list.)

Ironside, H. A.: *Addresses in the Song of Solomon.*

Beginning with Isaiah, and continuing through the Old Testament, there is a section of Scripture which is called the prophetic portion of the Bible. Although the predictive element bulks large in this section, the **prophets** were more than foretellers. Actually, they were men raised up of God in a decadent day when both priest and king were no longer worthy channels through which the expressions of God might flow.

These men not only spoke of events in the far off future but also spoke of local events in the immediate future. They had to speak in this manner in order to **qualify for** this **office** under God according to the Mosaic code (Deut. 18:20-22).

If the local event did not transpire just as the prophet predicted, he was labeled a false prophet and so treated. You may be sure that the message of the false prophet is not in the library of inspired Scripture. The prophetic books are filled with events that are local and fulfilled. A sharp distinction needs to be drawn between this portion and that which is yet to be fulfilled.

One of the greatest evidences of the fact that these men were speaking the words of God is revealed in the hundreds of prophecies that have been **fulfilled literally.** Man cannot guess the future. Even the weather man has difficulty in prognosticating the weather for twenty-four hours in advance although he has the advantage of all sorts of scientific and mechanical devices to assist him. No **modern weather man** could have been an accepted prophet in Israel. The law of compound probability forbids man from consistently foretelling the future. Each uncertain element which he adds decreases his chance of accuracy fifty per cent. The example of hundreds of prophecies which have had literal fulfillment has a genuine appeal to the honest mind and sincere seeker after the truth. Fulfilled prophecy is one of the infallible proofs of plenary verbal inspiration of Scripture.

The predictive element is the peculiar and particular contribution of these men of God. This does not mean there was not this element before them or after them. The last book of the Bible closes the message of God for the future.

The prophets were extremely **nationalistic.** They rebuked sin in high places as well as low. They warned the nation. They pleaded with a proud people to humble themselves and return to God. Fire and tears were mingled in their message, which was not one of doom and **gloom** alone, for they saw the Day of the Lord and the **glory** to follow. All of them looked through the darkness to the dawn of a new day. In the night of sin they saw the light of a coming Saviour and Sovereign; they saw the Millennial Kingdom coming in all its fulness. Their message must be interpreted before an appreciation of the Kingdom in the New Testament can be attained. The correct perspective of the Kingdom must be gained through the eyes of the Old Testament prophets.

The prophets were not supermen, they were men of like passions as we are, but having spoken for God, their message is still the **infallible** and inspired **Word** of God (1 Peter 1:10, 11 and 2 Peter 1:19-21).

Sweet is the harp of prophecy; too sweet not to be wronged by a mere mortal touch. (Cowper.)

ISAIAH

WRITER:

Isaiah, son of Amoz (1:1), was a royal prophet, if tradition is accurate. There is a Jewish tradition that his father was a son of King Joash and that his brother was King Amaziah.

There is another tradition that the reference in Hebrews 11:37 ("they were sawn asunder") refers to the death of Isaiah, and that King Manasseh was the one responsible for his execution in this way.

While this may or may not be accurate, it is true that the so-called higher critics have "sawn asunder" this prophet as being the writer of the book. They have fabricated the ghastly theory that there are several Isaiahs. According to this theory the book was produced by ghost writers whom they have labeled "Deutero-Isaiah" and "Trito-Isaiah." The book will not yield to being "sawn asunder" in this manner, for the New Testament quotes from all sections of the book and gives credit to one Isaiah.

THEME:

Isaiah means "The Salvation of Jehovah," which is the theme of the book. Isaiah is an illustration of I Peter 1:10-12. He has been called the Fifth Evangelist, the Prophet of Redemption, and the Messianic Prophet. The book has been labeled "The Gospel According to Isaiah." Christ's virgin birth, His character, His life, His death, His resurrection, and His second coming are all presented in Isaiah with definiteness and clarity.

OUTLINE:

I. **JUDGMENT** (Poetry), **chs. 1-35**
   Revelation of the Sovereign on the Throne
   (The Crown, chapter 6. The Government of God.)

   1. Solemn Call to the Universe to Come into the Court Room to Hear God's **Charge** Against the Nation Israel, ch. 1
   2. **Preview of the Future** for Judah and Jerusalem, ch. 2

3. **Present View** of Judah and Jerusalem, ch. 3
4. **Another Preview** of the Future, ch. 4
5. **Parable** of the Vineyard and Woes Predicted on Israel, ch. 5
6. Isaiah's **Personal Call** and Commission as Prophet, ch. 6
7. **Prediction** of Local and Far Events, chs. 7-10
   (Hope of Future in Coming Child)
8. **Millennial Kingdom,** chs. 11, 12
9. **Burdens of** Surrounding Nations (largely fulfilled), chs. 13-23
   (1) Burden of **Babylon,** chs. 13-14
   (2) Burden of **Moab,** chs. 15, 16
   (3) Burden of **Damascus,** ch. 17
   (4) Burden of the Land Beyond the Rivers of **Ethiopia,** ch. 18
   (5) Burden of **Egypt,** chs. 19, 20
   (6) Burden of **Babylon, Edom, Arabia,** ch. 21
   (7) Burden of the **Valley of Vision,** ch. 22
   (8) Burden of **Tyre,** ch. 23

10. **Kingdom, Process and Program** by which the Throne is Established on Earth, chs. 24-34
11. **Kingdom, Mundane Blessings** of the Millennium, ch. 35

II. HISTORIC INTERLUDE (Prose), chs. 36-39
(This section is probably a prophetic picture of how God will deliver His people in the Great Tribulation, see II Kings 18, 19; II Chron. 29, 30).

1. King **Hezekiah and the Invasion**
   of Sennacherib, King of Assyria, ch. 36
2. King **Hezekiah's Prayer**
   and the Destruction of the Assyrian Hosts, ch. 37
3. King **Hezekiah's Sickness,** Prayer and Healing, ch. 38
4. King **Hezekiah** Plays the **Fool,** ch. 39

III. SALVATION (Poetry), chs. 40-66
Revelation of the Saviour in the Place of Suffering
(The Cross, chapter 53. The Grace of God.)

(There is a threefold division marked by the concluding thought in each division, "There is no peace to the wicked.")

1. **Comfort of Jehovah**
   Which Comes Through the Servant, chs. 40-48
   (Polemic Against Idolatry—Help and Hope Come Only Through the Servant)
2. **Salvation of Jehovah**
   Which Comes Through the Suffering Servant, chs. 49-57

   (1) Redeemer of the Whole World,
       Who is God's **Servant,** chs. 49-52:12
   (2) Redemption Wrought by the Suffering Servant,
       Who Is God's **Sheep** (Lamb), chs. 52:13-53
   (3) Results of the Redemption Wrought by the Redeemer,
       Who Is God's Only **Saviour,** chs. 54-57

3. **Glory of Jehovah**
   Which Comes Through the Suffering Servant, chs. 58-66

   (1) Sin Hinders
       the Manifestation of the Glory of God, chs. 58, 59
   (2) Redeemer Is Coming to Zion, chs. 60-66
       (Nothing Can Hinder God's Progress—He Will Judge Sin)

RECOMMENDED BOOKS:

(See Genesis list.)

Jennings, F. C.: *Studies in Isaiah.*
McGee, J. Vernon: *Initiation Into Isaiah,* Vols. 1 & 2.
Vine, W. E.: *Isaiah.*

JEREMIAH

WRITER: Jeremiah, "the prophet of the broken heart."

HIS LIFE:

His book is partly autobiographical since he gave us so much of his personal history:

1. Born a priest in Anathoth, north of Jerusalem (1:1).
2. Chosen to be a prophet before he was born (1:5).
3. Called to the prophetic office while very young (1:6).
4. Commissioned (1:9, 10).
5. Began his ministry during the reign of King Josiah, and was a mourner at his funeral (2 Chron. 35:25).
6. Forbidden to marry because of the terrible times (16:1-4).
7. Converted no one, and was rejected by his people (11:18-21; 12:6; 18:17), hated, beaten, put in stocks (20:1-3), imprisoned (37:11-16), charged with being a traitor.
8. His message broke his own heart (9:1).
9. Wanted to resign but could not (20:9).
10. Saw the destruction of Jerusalem and the Babylonian captivity. Was permitted to remain in the land by the captain of the Babylonian forces. When the remnant wanted to flee to Egypt, Jeremiah prophesied against it (42:15-43:3), was forced to go with the remnant to Egypt (43:6, 7), and died there. Tradition says that he was stoned by the remnant.

HIS PERSONALITY:

God chose this man, who had a mother's heart, a trembling voice, and tear-filled eyes, to deliver a harsh message of judgment. The message that he gave broke his own heart.

One author has written, "He was not a man mighty as Elijah, eloquent as Isaiah, or seraphic as Ezekiel, but one who was timid and shrinking, conscious of his helplessness, yearning for a sympathy and love he was never to know—such was the chosen organ through which the Word of the Lord came to that corrupt and degenerate age."

The Lord Jesus Christ, weeping over Jerusalem, was a perfect fulfillment of Jeremiah.

HIS MESSAGE:

The message of Jeremiah was the most unwelcome ever delivered to a people. He was called a traitor because he said that they were to yield to Babylon (38:17-23). Isaiah, almost a century before him, had said to resist. Why this change? In Jeremiah's day there was only one thing left to do—surrender. In the economy of God, the nation was through, and (15:1) the "Times of the Gentiles" had already begun with Babylon, the head of gold (cp. Daniel 2).

Jeremiah predicted the 70 years captivity in Babylon (25: 9-12). However, he saw beyond the darkness to the light, and no prophet spoke so glowingly of the future as did he (23:3-8; 30; 31; 33:15-22).

The message of Jeremiah was not only unwelcome, but it was rejected by the nation (26:8-16).

KEY WORDS:

Backsliding (occurs 13 times—used only 4 other times in the Old Testament [Proverbs once, Hosea three times]).
Babylon (occurs 164 times—more than in the rest of Scripture combined).

OUTLINE:

(Difficult to outline because there is no logical or chronological order.)

 I. **Call of Prophet** During Reign of Josiah, **ch. 1**

 II. **Prophecies to Judah & Jerusalem**
   Prior to Zedekiah's Reign, **chs. 2-20**

   1. Twofold Condemnation of Judah, chs. 2-3:5
      (1) Rejected Jehovah
      (2) Reared Their Own Gods

3. To Egypt, ch. 46
4. To Philistia, ch. 47
5. To Moab, ch. 48
6. To Ammon, Edom, Damascus, Kedar, Hazor, Elam, ch. 49
7. To Babylon, chs. 50, 51

VII. **Fulfillment of Prophesied Destruction of Jerusalem, ch. 52**

RECOMMENDED BOOKS:

(See Genesis list.)

Ironside, H. A.: *Jeremiah, the Weeping Prophet.*
Morgan, G. Campbell: *Studies in the Prophecy of Jeremiah.*

LAMENTATIONS

WRITER: Jeremiah

ESTIMATION:

"There is nothing like the Lamentations of Jeremiah in the whole world. There has been plenty of sorrow in every age, and in every land, but such another preacher and author, with such a heart for sorrow, has never again been born. Dante comes next to Jeremiah, and we know that Jeremiah was the great exile's favorite prophet." (Whyte)

The book is filled with tears and sorrow. It is a paean of pain, a poem of pity, a proverb of pathos, a hymn of heartbreak, a psalm of sadness, a symphony of sorrow, a story of sifting, a tale of tears, a dirge of desolation, a tragedy of travail, an account of agony, and a book of "boo-hoo." It is the wailing wall of the Bible.

KEY VERSE: Lam. 1:18

It explains the reason that Jerusalem is in ruins.

FEATURE:

Jeremiah reminds us of Another as He sat weeping over Jerusalem. The only difference is that Jerusalem was in ruins and the Temple burned as Jeremiah gazed upon the debris. Jesus, about 6 centuries later, wept over the city because of what was going to happen.

> To Jeremiah the destruction of Jerusalem was a matter of history.
> To Jesus the destruction of Jerusalem was a matter of prophecy.

No blues singer ever sang a sadder song than Jeremiah. Lamentations is composed of 5 of his sad songs which are elegies.

OUTLINE:

I. Elegy, ch. 1

A call to consider the destruction of Jerusalem;
The reason for the frightful destruction (vv. 8, 18);

An invitation to all to enter into the sorrow of the prophet
(v. 12).

II. Elegy, ch. 2

Doleful details of the effect of the judgment of God upon the remnant that remain (v. 10);

The elation of the enemy from without (v. 15).

III. Elegy, ch. 3

The tragic and catastrophic destruction of Jerusalem would have been total had it not been for the mercies and faithfulness of God.

IV. Elegy, ch. 4

Contrast between the former state of prosperity and the present state of Jerusalem in poverty.

V. Elegy, ch. 5

A cry to God to remember the nation Israel. "Prayer of Jeremiah."

RECOMMENDED BOOKS:

(See Genesis list.)

EZEKIEL

WRITER: Ezekiel

Ezekiel was a priest (1:3), but never served in that office, as he was taken captive during the reign of Jehoiachin (2 Ki. 24:10-16) at about the former's 25th year. Daniel had been taken captive in the first captivity during Jehoiakim's reign, about 8 years before Ezekiel was taken captive.

Ezekiel was contemporary with Jeremiah and Daniel. Jeremiah was an old man who spoke to the remnant that remained in the land; Daniel spoke to the court of the king of Babylon; Ezekiel spoke to the captives who had been brought to the rivers of Babylon. While the other captives were weeping when they remembered Zion, Ezekiel was exulting in the greatest visions ever given to any prophet.

HIS MESSAGE:

His message was the most spiritual of the prophets as he dealt more with the person of God. Someone has said, "Ezekiel is the prophet of the Spirit, as Isaiah is the prophet of the Son, and Jeremiah the prophet of the Father."

During the first years of the captivity the false prophets said that the people would be returned to Jerusalem, and that the city would not be destroyed. It was not until the final deportation, during Zedekiah's reign, that the city was destroyed—some 11 years after Ezekiel was taken captive.

Jeremiah had sent a message to Babylon (Jer. 29) saying that the city would be destroyed. Ezekiel confirmed this message, and warned the people that they must turn to God before they could return to Jerusalem.

Ezekiel began his ministry 5 years after his captivity when he was about 30 years old.

HIS METHOD:

In many ways he spoke in the darkest days of the nation. He

stood at the bottom of the valley in the darkest corner. He had to meet the false hope given by the false prophets and the indifference and the despondency begotten in the days of sin and disaster. The people would not listen to him or to his message. Therefore, he resorted to a new method. Instead of *speaking* in parables, he acted them out (24:24). We have had "flagpole sitters" and walkathons" in our day which attracted the attention of the public. This sort of thing was the method of Ezekiel and is indicative of a day of decay.

HIS MEANING:

Ezekiel is the prophet of the glory of the Lord. Three prophets of Israel spoke when they were out of the land: Ezekiel, Daniel, and John. Each has written an apocalypse. Although they used highly symbolic language, they saw the brightest light and held the highest hope. Ezekiel saw the Shekinah glory of the Lord leave Solomon's Temple, and he saw the return of the glory of the Lord which was projected into the future during the Kingdom.

The meaning of Ezekiel is seen in the coming glory during the Kingdom. Ezekiel looked beyond the sufferings of Christ to "the glory that should follow" (1 Peter 1:11).

OUTLINE:

I. Glory of the Lord; Commission of the Prophet, chs. 1-7

1. Display of the Glory, ch. 1
2. Prophet's Call & Enduement with Power for the Office, ch. 2
3. Prophet's Preparation; Office as Watchman, ch. 3
4. Judgment of Jerusalem, ch. 4
5. Sign of Prophet Shaving Hair, ch. 5
6. Sword to Fall upon Jerusalem; Remnant to be Saved, ch. 6
7. Prophecy of Final Destruction of Jerusalem, ch. 7

II. Glory of the Lord; Complete Captivity of Jerusalem & Israel; Departure of the Glory, chs. 8-24

1. Vision of the Glory; Temple Defilement by Idolatry Explains its Destruction, ch. 8
2. Shekinah Glory Prepares to Leave Temple, ch. 9

3. Shekinah Glory Fills Holy Place; Leaves the Temple, ch. 10
4. Prophecy against Rulers of Jerusalem, ch. 11
5. Ezekiel Enacts Destruction of Jerusalem, ch. 12
6. Prophecy against Pseudo-Prophets & Prophetesses, ch. 13
7. Prophecy against Idolatry of Elders;
   Certain Destruction of Jerusalem, ch. 14
8. Vision of the Vine, ch. 15
9. Jerusalem Likened to
   Abandoned Baby Adopted by God, ch. 16
10. Riddle of 2 Eagles, ch. 17
11. Wages of Sin is Death, ch. 18
12. Elegy of Jehovah over Princes of Israel, ch. 19
13. Review of Sins of Nation;
    Future Judgment & Restoration, ch. 20
14. King of Babylon to Remove Last King
    of Davidic Line Until Messiah Comes, ch. 21
15. Review of Abominations of Jerusalem, ch. 22
16. Parable of 2 Sisters (Samaria & Jerusalem), ch. 23
17. Parable of Boiling Pot, ch. 24

III. Glory of the Lord; Judgment of Nations, chs. 25-32

1. Against Ammon, Moab, Edom, Philistia, ch. 25
2. Against Tyre, chs. 26-28
3. Against Egypt, chs. 29-32

IV. Glory of the Lord & Coming Kingdom, chs. 33-48

1. Recommission of the Prophet, chs. 33, 34
2. Restoration of Israel, chs. 35, 36
3. Resurrection of Israel, ch. 37
4. Repudiation of Gog & Magog, chs. 38, 39
5. Rebuilt Temple, chs. 40-42
6. Return of Glory of the Lord, chs. 43-48

RECOMMENDED BOOKS:

Gaebelein, A. C.: *The Prophet Ezekiel.*
Ironside, H. A.: *Ezekiel the Prophet.*
Sale-Harrison, L.: *The Coming Great Northern Confederacy.*
The Numerical Bible: *Ezekiel.*

DANIEL

WRITER: Daniel

We know more of Daniel, the man, than we do of any other prophet. He gives us a personal account of his life from the time he was carried captive to Babylon in the third year of Jehoiakim's reign, about 606 B.C. (1:1), until the first year of King Cyrus, about 536 B.C. (1:21). (See also 9:2.) Daniel's life and ministry bridge the entire 70 years captivity. At the beginning of the book he is a boy in his teens; at the end he is an old man of fourscore or more years.

God's estimate of Daniel: "O Daniel, a man greatly beloved" (10:11). Three words characterize Daniel's life: *purpose, prayer* and *prophecy*.

DATE: 6th Century B.C.

It was written between the third year of Nebuchadnezzar's reign, about 606 B.C. (1:1) and the first year of Cyrus, about 536 B.C. (1:21).

This early dating has been maintained successfully by conservative scholars against the massed onslaught of liberalism. Porphyry, a heretic in the 3rd Century A.D., declared the book of Daniel was a forgery, written during the time of Antiochus Epiphanes and the Maccabees (170 B.C.)—almost 400 years after Daniel had lived. However, the Septuagint, the Greek version of the Old Testament which was written prior to the time of Antiochus Epiphanes, contains the book of Daniel. And the historian Josephus records an incident during the time of Alexander the Great, which supports the early authorship. Also Daniel's contemporary, Ezekiel, who was with the captives, made reference to the character of Daniel (14:14, 20), and to his office as prophet (28:3), which is conclusive evidence against the theory that this book belongs to the Maccabean period. Finally, the Lord Jesus Christ spoke of Daniel "the prophet" (Matt. 24:15; Mk. 13:14). His endorsement is valid and sufficient for every believer whether or not he has examined the arguments of the critics.

Daniel

HIS MESSAGE:

Daniel is the prophet of "the times of the Gentiles." The major portion of his prophecies was directly concerned with the Gentile nations. The notable exception is Daniel 9 which concerns the 70 weeks, but here the emphasis is upon the interval after the cutting off of the Messiah between the 69th and the 70th weeks. It is during this period that the city and sanctuary are destroyed, and the "times of the Gentiles" is identified as the time when "Jerusalem shall be trodden down of the Gentiles." Evidently, the wise men from the east (Matt. 2:1) knew the prophecy of Daniel. A portion of the book of Daniel was written in Aramaic, the language of the Gentiles of that day. All of this does not infer that the book was not written for Israel. On the contrary, the Jews were acquainted with the prophesies of Daniel in his day (Ezek. 28:3).

THEME: Dan. 2:44

Dr. G. Campbell Morgan gave this theme: "Persistent Government of God in the Government of the World." This is the book of the universal sovereignty of God. Prophecy is interwoven with history to show that God is overruling the idolatry, blasphemy, self-will and intolerance of the Gentiles.

OUTLINE:

I. The **HISTORIC NIGHT** with **PROPHETIC LIGHT**, chs. 1-6

    A. **Decline** of Judah; **Fall** of Jerusalem. Daniel Taken Captive to Babylon; His **Decision** to be True to God, ch. 1

    B. **Dream of Nebuchadnezzar** about a Multi-Metallic **Image;** Interpretation by Daniel Concerning the Four Kingdoms of "the Times of the Gentiles," ch. 2

    C. **Decree of Nebuchadnezzar** to Enforce **Universal Idolatry;** Three Hebrews Cast into the Furnace for Refusal to Bow to Image of Gold, ch. 3

    D. **Dream of Nebuchadnezzar** about a Great **Tree** Hewn Down to a Stump; Fulfilled in Subsequent Period of Madness of the King, ch. 4

    E. **Downfall of Babylon Foretold** by Daniel as He Read Handwriting on Wall at the Feast of Belshazzar, ch. 5

F. **Decree of Darius,** the Median, to Enforce
Worship of Himself; Daniel Cast into Den
of Lions for Praying to the God of Heaven, ch. 6

II. PROPHETIC LIGHT in the HISTORIC NIGHT, chs. 7-12

A. **Daniel's Vision** of **Four Beasts** Concerning Four Kingdoms
of "the Times of the Gentiles", ch. 7
B. **Daniel's Vision** of **Ram** and **He Goat**
and Another Little Horn, ch. 8
C. **Daniel's Vision** of **Seventy Weeks**
Concerning Nation Israel, ch. 9
D. **Daniel's Vision** Relating to Israel in **Immediate Future**
and **Latter Days;** Historical Little Horn
and Little Horn of the Latter Days, chs. 10-12
1. **Preparation** for Vision by Prayer of Daniel;
Appearance of Heavenly Messenger, ch. 10
2. **Prophecy** Concerning Persia and Grecia,
Historical "Little Horn";
Eschatological "Little Horn", ch. 11
3. **Preview** of Israel in Latter Days; Great Tribulation;
Resurrection; Rewards;
Final Word about The End Times, ch. 12

An outline which is closer to the text and the purpose of the
book should also be given. The Old Testament is written in the
Hebrew language, with but one exception—a portion of the book
of Daniel. From chapter two, verse four, through chapter seven,
Daniel is in Aramaic, the Gentile and diplomatic language of
Daniel's day. This section deals exclusively with "the times of the
Gentiles." The remainder of the book correlates the nation Israel
with this program. The book of Daniel deals with Gentiles and
Jews—the Church is totally excluded. This book is first to the Gen-
tiles and also to the Jews.

With this in mind, note the following brief outline.

1. **Introduction** 1:1-2:3
(The Private Life of Daniel)
2. The **Panoramic Portrayal** of the Times of the Gentiles 2:4-7:28
(The Public Life of Daniel)
3. The **Prophetic History** of the Nation
Israel to the Millennium, chs. 8-12
(The Prophetic Visions of Daniel)

Daniel

RECOMMENDED BOOKS:

Culver, Robert: *Daniel and the Latter Days.*
Gaebelein, A. C.: *The Prophet Daniel.*
Ironside, H. A.: *Lectures on Daniel The Prophet.*
Kelly, William: *Lectures on the Book of Daniel.*
McGee, J. Vernon: *Delving Through Daniel.*
Pettingill, W. L.: *Simple Studies in Daniel.*
Ritchie, John: *The Book of Daniel.*
Sale-Harrison, L.: *The Resurrection of the Old Roman Empire.*

HOSEA

Beginning with Hosea and concluding with Malachi, there are 12 short prophecies called the Minor Prophets. They are so called because of the size of the books and not because of their content. The Minor Prophets all dealt with the same major issues of the Major Prophets. They were actually quoted by the Major Prophets (Jer. 26:18). The Minor Prophets were exceedingly nationalistic, but they were not isolationists. There were to be no godless alliances with other nations, but they were warned of an isolationism from God. They were extremely patriotic, and denounced political and moral corruption. This has given rise to the modern emphasis on the social message of the prophets.

It is a striking fact that there is scant reference material on the Minor Prophets. A cursory inspection of any religious library will corroborate this. There is a wealth of material on most of the books of the Bible, but when you leave Daniel and pass over to Hosea, it is like going from a fertile valley to a sterile desert.

WRITER: Hosea

All that is known of him is what he reveals in his prophecy.

THE TIME: Hos. 1:1

In spite of the fact that Hosea mentions the four kings of Judah first, and the one king of Israel last, he was a prophet to the Northern Kingdom, as the content of the book reveals. He was contemporary with Amos, another prophet to Israel, and also contemporary with Micah and Isaiah, prophets to Judah. His ministry extended over half a century, and he lived to see the fulfillment of his prophecy in the captivity of Israel.

THE THEME: "Return unto the Lord" (Hos. 6:1)

"Return" occurs 15 times.

Hosea

"Ephraim" occurs 36 times.

"Backsliding" occurs 3 times. Hosea and Jeremiah are the two prophets who talk about backsliding and the cure for it.

What Jeremiah was to Judah at the time of the captivity of the southern kingdom, Hosea was to Israel, over a century before, at the time of the captivity of the northern kingdom. Both spoke out of a heartbreaking personal experience.

PERSONAL EXPERIENCE:

Hosea's experience was in the home while Jeremiah's was in the nation. Jeremiah was commanded not to marry. Hosea was commanded to marry a harlot, or, as he brutally stated the case, "a wife of whoredoms." He married Gomer, and she bore him two sons and a daughter. Afterward she played the harlot again, and Hosea put her out of his home. But God commanded him to go and to take this unfaithful harlot and to bring her back into his home and to love her again. "Now," God said in effect to Hosea, "you are prepared to speak for me to Israel—Israel has played the harlot, but I love her and will yet bring her back into her homeland."

OUTLINE:

I. PERSONAL—
The Prophet and His Faithless Wife, Gomer, chs. 1-3

1. Marriage of Hosea and Gomer, the Harlot, ch. 1
2. Gomer Proves Faithless;
   Israel Proves Faithless; God Proves Faithful, ch. 2
3. Hosea Commanded to Take Gomer Again, ch. 3

II. PROPHETIC—
The Lord and the Faithless Nation Israel, chs. 4-14

1. Israel **Plays the Harlot,** chs. 4, 5

   (1) Israel Guilty of Lawlessness, Immorality,
       Ignorance of God's Word, and Idolatry, ch. 4
   (2) Israel Turns from God; God Turns from Israel;
       Deterioration within Follows. ch. 5

2. Israel (Ephraim) **Will Return in the Last Days;**
      Presently to be Judged for Current Sins, ch. 6

3. Israel (Ephraim) **Could Escape Judgment** by Turning to God
      Who Loves Her (Key: v.8), chs. 7-12

      (1) Israel (Silly Dove) Turns to Egypt and Assyria, ch. 7
      (2) Israel Turns to Golden Calves and Altars of Sin, ch. 8
      (3) Israel (Backsliding Heifer) Turns to Land Productivity;
          Will be Driven from Land, chs. 9, 10
      (4) Israel Turns from God—Must be Judged;
          God Will Not Give Her Up, chs. 11, 12

4. Israel (Ephraim) **Will Turn from Idols to God** in Last Days,
      chs. 13, 14

      (1) Israel Will Be Judged in the Present, ch. 13
      (2) Israel Will Be Saved in the Future, ch. 14

RECOMMENDED BOOKS:

Barker, H. P.: *Christ in the Minor Prophets.*
Feinberg, Charles L.: *God's Love for Israel.*
Gaebelein, A. C.: *The Annotated Bible, Vol. V.*
Ironside, H. A.: *Minor Prophets.*
Pusey, E. B.: *Minor Prophets.*

JOEL

WRITER: Joel

Nothing is known of this prophet except what is given in the opening verse. His name means *Jehovah is God.*

THE TIME:

Considered by many to be the earliest of the writing prophets, he was a prophet to Judah probably about the time of the reign of Joash, king of Judah. He probably knew Elijah and Elisha. The critical school, adopting their usual custom, have placed this book at the other extreme, even after the captivity.

THE THEME:

"The day of the LORD" (1:15; 2:1, 11, 31; 3:14)

FEATURES:

1. "The day of the LORD" or "the day of Jehovah" is an expression introduced by Joel (if he is the first of the writing prophets [there are about 50 prophets in all]). From the mountain top of the beginning of written prophecy he saw the furthest into the future. "The day of the LORD" is an expression that is freighted with meaning. It seems to include not only the coming Millennial Kingdom, but also to include all the judgments which precede the setting up of the Kingdom and the return of Christ.

2. His description of a literal plague of locusts, and its comparison with future judgments is dramatic and a literary gem.

3. He is the prophet who mentioned the outpouring of the Holy Spirit, which was referred to by Peter on the day of Pentecost.

OUTLINE:

I. Literal and Local PLAGUE of LOCUSTS, ch. 1:1-14
II. Looking to the DAY OF THE LORD (Prelude), chs. 1:15-2:32

III.   Looking at the DAY OF THE LORD (Postlude), ch. 3

1. The Great Tribulation, vv. 1-15
2. The Millennial Kingdom, vv. 16-21

RECOMMENDED BOOKS:

Gaebelein, A. C.: *The Prophet Joel.*

AMOS

WRITER: Amos

Amos was not a graduate of the school of the prophets, but was a layman. He was a herdsman and a gatherer of sycamore fruit (1:1; 7:14, 15). He was a native of Tekoa (1:1), a villáge about 12 miles south of Jerusalem. Although born in Judea, his messages were to the Northern Kingdom of Israel primarily, and to the world in general, as the text indicates.

TIME:

His ministry was during the reign of Jeroboam II, king of Israel, and Uzziah, king of Judah. He was a contemporary of Hosea in Israel and of Isaiah and Micah in Judah. The exact time was "two years before the earthquake" (1:1). This earthquake was of such proportions that Zechariah mentioned it 200 years later (Zech. 14:5), and identified it as having come during the reign of Uzziah.

THEME:

Amos presented God as the ruler of this world, and declared that all nations were responsible to Him. The measure of responsibility is created by the light which a nation has. The final test for any nation (or individual) is found in 3:3: "Can two walk together, except they be agreed?" In a day of prosperity, he pronounced punishment. Judgment of God awaited nations living in luxury and lolling in immorality.

OUTLINE:

I. JUDGMENT on SURROUNDING NATIONS, chs. 1:1-2:3

1. Introduction, 1:1, 2
2. Judgment against **Syria** for Cruelty, 1:3-5
3. Judgment against **Philistia** for Making Slaves, 1:6-8
4. Judgment against **Phoenicia** for Breaking Treaty, 1:9, 10
5. Judgment against **Edom** for Revengeful Spirit, 1:11, 12
6. Judgment against **Ammon** for Violent Crimes, 1:13-15
7. Judgment against **Moab** for Injustice, 2:1-3

II. JUDGMENT on JUDAH and ISRAEL, chs. 2:4-6:14

1. Judgment against **Judah** for Despising Law, 2:4, 5
2. Judgment against **Israel** for Immorality and Blasphemy, 2:6-16
3. God's Charge against Whole House of Israel (12 Tribes), ch. 3
   (Privilege creates responsibility; the higher the blessing, the greater the punishment.)
4. Israel Punished in **Past** for Iniquity, ch. 4
5. Israel Will Be Punished in **Future** for Iniquity, ch. 5
6. Israel Admonished in **Present** to Depart from Iniquity, ch. 6

III. VISIONS of FUTURE, chs. 7-9

1. Vision of **Grasshoppers,** 7:1-3
2. Vision of **Fire,** 7:4-6
3. Vision of **Plumbline,** 7:7-9
4. Historic Interlude, 7:10-17
   (Personal Experience of Prophet.)
5. Vision of Basket of **Summer Fruit,** ch. 8
6. Vision of World-Wide **Dispersion,** 9:1-10
7. Vision of World-Wide **Regathering & Restoration of Kingdom,** 9:11-15

RECOMMENDED BOOKS:

(See Genesis; Hosea)

Havner, Vance: *Amos, The Prophet with a Modern Message.*

OBADIAH

WRITER: Obadiah

Obadiah means "Servant of Jehovah." He is one of four prophets about whom we know absolutely nothing, except that he wrote prophecy. The other three prophets are Habakkuk, Haggai, and Malachi. Obadiah is like a ghost writer—he is there but we do not know him. He lived up to his name. A servant boasts of no genealogy, neither exploits nor experiences. Dr. Pusey said, "God has willed that his name alone and this brief prophecy should be known to the world."

DATE:

There is a great difference of opinion as to the date of this prophet. There are some who give the date of 887 B.C., which fixes the time during the reign of Jehoram and the bloody Athaliah (2 Ki. 8:18; cp. 11:1-16). Dr. Pusey placed it during the reign of Jehoshaphat (2 Chr. 17:7). If this is accurate, we have one isolated reference to Obadiah in history. Nevertheless, this name was as common in that day as the name *John* is today. Canon Farrar gave the date as 587 B.C. Dr. Moorehead concurred in this, as he suggested that Obadiah was probably a contemporary with Jeremiah. The whole question seems to hinge on verse 11. Is this verse historical or prophetical? The natural interpretation is the historical one, which would give it the late date. Most likely it was written subsequent to the Babylonian captivity.

KEY: Edom, Obad. 6.

FEATURES:

Obadiah is the shortest book in the Old Testament—only one page, 21 verses. But the brevity of the message does not render it less important or less significant for us today. Like the other minor prophets, the message is primary, it is pertinent, it is practical, and it is poignant. It is a message that can be geared into this day in which we are living.

Obadiah tells us immediately, bluntly and to the point, "Thus saith the Lord GOD concerning Edom...." It is the prophecy of judgment against Edom.

BACKGROUND:

The Edomites were those who were descended from Esau, just as the Israelites are those who are descended from Jacob.

The story of Esau and Jacob is that of twin brothers, sons of Isaac and Rebekah. They were not identical twins, actually they were opposites (see Gen. 25:24-34).

Esau despised his birthright. The man who had the birthright was in contact with God, he was the priest of his family, he was the man who had a covenant from God, the man who had a relationship with God. In effect Esau said, "I would rather have a bowl of soup than have a relationship with God."

Having seen Esau in the first book of the Old Testament, look now at the last book of the Old Testament and read this strange language:

> I have loved you, saith the LORD. Yet ye say, In what way hast thou loved us? Was not Esau Jacob's brother? saith the LORD; yet I loved Jacob, and I hated Esau...
> [Mal. 1:2, 3a].

This is a strange thing for God to say—"I loved Jacob and I hated Esau." The explanation is in the little book of Obadiah.

OUTLINE:

I. EDOM — DESTRUCTION, vv. 1-16

1. **Charge** against Edom, vv. 1-9
2. **Crime** of Edom, vv. 10-14
3. **Catastrophe** to Edom, vv. 15, 16
   (Poetic justice [*lex talionis*] — law of retaliation)

II. ISRAEL — RESTORATION, vv. 17-21

1. **Condition** of Israel, v. 17
2. **Calling** of Israel, v. 18
3. **Consummation** of All Things, vv. 19-21
   (*"And the kingdom shall be the Lord's"*)

Obadiah

RECOMMENDED BOOKS:

(See Genesis; Hosea)

Gaebelein, Frank E.: *The Servant and The Dove.*

JONAH

Is the book of Jonah the Achilles' heel of the Bible? It is, if we are to accept the ridiculous explanations of the critics. The translators of the Septuagint were the first to question its reasonableness. They set the pattern for the avalanche of criticism which was to follow. The ancient method of modernism is to allegorize the book and to classify it with *Robinson Crusoe* and *Gulliver's Travels.*

WRITER: Jonah

Jonah was an historical character. The historical record of the kings of Israel and Judah is accepted as reliable. Speaking of Jeroboam II, king of Israel, the historian records the name of Jonah (2 Ki. 14:25). Jeroboam was a real person, Israel was a real nation, Hamath was a real place, and it is unlikely that Jonah, the son of Amittai, was a figment of the imagination. Neither is it reasonable to say that this is another Jonah, that there were two Jonahs whose fathers were named Amittai and whose offices were prophets (especially since it is not a common name). Obviously the Lord Jesus considered Jonah a real person, and He accepted the record of the book of Jonah as true (Lk. 11:30 and Matt. 12:39-41).

DATE: Between 800 and 750 B.C.

Conservative scholars place the writing of this book before 745 B.C. The incidents took place about that time. Some even place it as early as 860 B.C. It seems best to place it between 800 and 750 B.C. Students of history will recognize this as the period when Nineveh was in its heyday, and the nation of Assyria was at its zenith also. It was destroyed by 606 B.C. By the time of Herodatus the city of Nimrod had ceased to exist. When Xenaphon passed the city, it was deserted but he testified that the walls still stood and they were 150 feet high. Historians now estimate they were at least 100 feet high and 40 feet thick.

REMARKS:

Properly speaking, the book of Jonah is not a prophecy, and seems to be out of step among the minor prophets. It contains no prophecy, although Jonah was a prophet. It is the personal account of a major event in the life of Jonah. As the narrator, he told of his experience which was a sign of the greatest event in the history of the world—*the resurrection of Jesus Christ.*

Keep in mind that the fish is not the hero of the story—neither is it the villain. The book is not even about a fish. The chief difficulty is in keeping a correct perspective. The fish is among the props and does not occupy the star's dressing room. Let us distinguish between the essentials and the incidentals. The incidentals are the fish, the gourd, the east wind, the boat, and Nineveh. The essentials are Jehovah and Jonah—God and man.

SIGNIFICANT SUBJECTS:

1. This is the one book of the Old Testament which **sets forth the resurrection.** When a wicked and adulterous generation was seeking after a sign, Jesus referred them to the book of Jonah for the message: "As Jonah...so Jesus."

2. **Salvation is not by works.** Salvation is by faith which leads to repentance. The book of Jonah is read by the orthodox Jews on the Great day of Atonement (Yom Kippur). One great self-evident truth from the ritual of this day is that the way to God was not by works, but by the blood of a substitutionary sacrifice provided by God. The most significant statement in the book of Jonah is in 2:9: "Salvation is of the Lord."

3. **God's purpose of grace cannot be frustrated.** If Jonah had refused to go to Nineveh the second time, God would have raised up another instrument, or, more likely, He would have had another fish ready to give Jonah the green signal toward Nineveh. The book shows God's determination to get His message of salvation to a people who will hear and accept it.

4. **God will not cast us aside for faithlessness.** When Jonah failed the first time, God did not give him up. The most encouraging words which a faltering and failing child of God can hear are, "And the word of the Lord came unto Jonah the second time."

5. **God is good and gracious.** The most penetrating picture of God in the entire Bible is in 4:2. It is wrong to say that the Old Testament reveals a God of wrath, and the New Testament

a God of love. He is no vengeful deity in the book of Jonah!

6. **God is the God of the Gentiles.** It has been suggested that Romans 3:29 be written over this book. It is the answer to the critics who declaim that the Old Testament presents a local and limited deity, a tribal deity. The book of Jonah is a great book on world missions.

When you consult a timetable in a railroad station or airport, there are 3 important factors you note: (1) destination, (2) departure time, (3) arrival time. It is possible to construct the 4 brief chapters of Jonah into the form of a timetable.

Timetable of the Book of Jonah

LEAVE	DESTINATION	ARRIVE	
Israel (Samaria or Gath-hepher)	Nineveh	Fish	Ch. 1
Fish	Nineveh	Dry Land	Ch. 2
Dry Land	Nineveh	Nineveh	Ch. 3
Nineveh	Gourd Vine	Heart of God	Ch. 4

RECOMMENDED BOOKS:

(See Genesis; Hosea)

Gaebelein, Frank E.: *The Servant and the Dove.*
McGee, J. Vernon: *Jonah, Dead or Alive?*

MICAH

WRITER: Micah

His name means *Who is like Jehovah?* The word has the same derivation as *Michael,* which means "Who is like God?" There are many Micahs in the Scripture, but this one is identified as a Morasthite (1:1), since he was an inhabitant of Moresheth-gath (1:14), a place about 20 miles southwest of Jerusalem, near Lachish. He is not to be confused with any other Micah of Scripture.

TIME:

Micah was a contemporary of Isaiah and prophesied during the reigns of Jotham, Ahaz, and Hezekiah (1:1). He was younger than Isaiah, and his prophecy might be called a miniature Isaiah or Isaiah in shorthand, since there are striking similarities. Ewald and Wellhausen attacked the unity of this book. It is the same attack which has been made against Isaiah.

The ministry of Micah was directed to both Jerusalem and Samaria (1:1), and he evidently saw the captivity of the Northern Kingdom.

THEME: The judgment and redemption of God, Mic. 7:18

God hates sin, but He loves the souls of the sinners.

STYLE:

For many this is the favorite of the minor prophets. The writing is pungent and personal. Micah was trenchant, touching, and tender. He was realistic and reportorial—he would have made a good war correspondent. There is an exquisite beauty about this brochure which combines God's infinite tenderness with His judgments. There are several famous passages which are familiar to the average Christian. Through the gloom of impending judgment, Micah saw clearly the coming glory of the redemption of Israel.

STRIKING STATEMENTS:

1:6-16—Assyria destroyed Samaria (a miniature of the great

destruction of the last days [4:11-13]).

2:12—The future regathering of the remnant.

3:6, 7—The end of prophecy.

3:12; 4:9, 10—Coming destruction of Jerusalem by Babylon and not by Assyria. Jeremiah's life was preserved because of 3:12 (Jer. 26:18).

4:1-8—The coming Kingdom over the entire earth (one world).

5:2—The birth of Christ (quoted in Matthew 2:5, 6).

5:7, 8—The future ministry of the remnant.

6:6-8—"One of the most sublime and impassioned declarations of spiritual religion that the Old Testament contains."
(Dean Stanley)

7:18, 19—Micah lived up to his name in exalting God. Dr. Pierson calls it, "...A little poem of 12 lines in the Hebrew...one of the most exquisite things to be found in the entire Old Testament."

REMARKS:

Micah pronounced judgment on the cities of Israel and Jerusalem in Judah. These centers influenced the people of the nation. These were the urban problems that sound very much like our present day problems. Micah condemns violence, corruption, robbery, covetousness, gross materialism, and spiritual bankruptcy. He could well be labeled "The prophet of the city."

OUTLINE:

The more natural division of the prophecy is to note that Micah gave 3 messages, each beginning with the injunction, "Hear" (1:2, 3:1, 6:1).

The first was addressed to "all people"; the second was addressed specifically to the leaders of Israel; the third was a personal word of pleading to Israel to repent and return to God.

Micah

"WHO IS A GOD LIKE UNTO THEE" IN:

I. PROCLAIMING Future Judgment for Past Sins, **chs. 1-3**

    1. Prophet's 1st Message Directed against Samaria,
       Reaches to Jerusalem, ch. 1
    2. Prophet's 2nd Message Describes Specific Sins, ch. 2
    3. Prophet's 3rd Message Denounces Leaders for Sins, ch. 3

II. PROPHESYING Future Glory
    Because of Past Promises, **chs. 4, 5**

    1. Prophecies of Last Days, ch. 4
    2. Prophecy of 1st Coming of Christ
       Before 2nd Coming and Kingdom, ch. 5

III. PLEADING Present Repentance
    Because of Past Redemption, **ch. 6**

IV. PARDONING All Iniquity
    Because of Who God Is and What He Does, **ch. 7**

RECOMMENDED BOOKS:

(See Genesis; Hosea)

NAHUM

Nahum means "comforter." Nahum is identified (1:1) as an El-koshite. This is all that is known of the writer of this book. Elkosh was a city in Assyria, a few miles north of the ruins of Nineveh. Nahum could well have lived there and have prophesied to Nineveh, as Daniel did to Babylon later on. The most likely explanation, however, is that there was a village by this name in Galilee. Jerome recorded that a guide pointed out to him such a village as the birthplace of Nahum—but this was a millennium after Nahum lived. Dr. John D. Davis gives the meaning for *Capernaum* as "the village of Nahum." If *Capernaum* is a Hebrew word, then this is the evident origin.

TIME:

There are many dates assigned to this book and this prophet. Dates are given anywhere from 720 to 636 B.C. by conservative scholars. It seems reasonable to locate him about 100 years after Jonah, and about 100 years before the destruction of Nineveh—between 606 and 612 B.C. He probably lived during the reign of Hezekiah, and saw the destruction of the Northern Kingdom.

THEME: The burden (judgment) of Nineveh (1:1).

MESSAGE:

Nahum sounds the death knell of Nineveh, and pronounces judgment, by total destruction, on Assyria. God was just in doing this. Jonah, almost a century before, had brought a message from God, and Nineveh had repented. However the repentance was transitory, and God patiently gave this new generation opportunity to repent (1:3). The day of grace ends, and the moment of doom comes (3:19). Assyria had served God's purpose (Isa. 10:5), and would be destroyed. The destruction of Nineveh according to the details which are given in this written prophecy is almost breathtaking.

This is a message of comfort to a people who live in fear of a powerful and godless nation. God will destroy any godless nation.

Nahum

Some folk think *Nahum* should be called *Ho-hum!* However, Nahum is a thrilling book to study. It reveals the other side of the attributes of God. God is love, but God is holy and righteous and good.

OUTLINE:

I. **Justice and Goodness of God, 1:1-8**

II. Justice and Goodness of God **Demonstrated in Decision** to Destroy Nineveh and to Give the Gospel, **1:9-15**

III. Justice and Goodness of God **Exhibited in Execution** of His Decision to Destroy Nineveh, **chs. 2,3**

1. Annihilation of Assyria, ch. 2

2. Avenging Action of God Justified, ch. 3

RECOMMENDED BOOKS:

(See Genesis; Hosea)

HABAKKUK

WRITER: Habakkuk

His name means *love's embrace.* Dr. A. C. Gaebelein has said, "Dr. Martin Luther gave a very striking definition of his name, which cannot be improved upon. 'Habakkuk signifies an embracer, or one who embraces another, takes him into his arms. He embraces his people, and takes them to his arms, i.e., he comforts them and holds them up, as one embraces a weeping child, to quiet it with the assurance that if God wills it shall soon be better.' "

This is all that is known of the writer, except that he was the doubting Thomas of the Old Testament. He had a question mark for a brain.

TIME:

Probably written during the reign of Josiah, about the time of the destruction of Nineveh, and the rise of Babylon to power. Habakkuk appeared in the twilight, just before the darkness of the captivity.

FORM:

The closing statement, "For the chief musician on my stringed instrument" (A.R.V.), reveals that this is a song. The last chapter is a psalm. The entire prophecy is a gem of beauty. It has been translated into a metric version by Dr. Gaebelein. Delitzsch wrote, "His language is classical throughout, full of rare and select turns and words." Moorehouse wrote, "It is distinguished for its magnificent poetry."

MESSAGE:

The book opens in gloom and closes in glory. It begins with an interrogation point and closes with an exclamation mark. Habakkuk is a big WHY? Why God permits evil is a question that every thoughtful mind has faced. This book is the answer to the question. Will God straighten out the injustice of the world? This book answers the question. Is God doing anything about the wrongs of the world? This book says that He is. The book is the personal experience of the prophet told in poetry, as Jonah's was told in prose.

THEME: Faith

Habakkuk has been called "the prophet of faith." The great statement of 2:4, "The just shall live by faith," has been quoted 3 times in the New Testament: Rom. 1:17; Gal. 3:11; Heb. 10:38.

OUTLINE:

I. PERPLEXITY of the Prophet, ch. 1

1. **1st Problem** of the Prophet, 1:1-4
   Why does God permit evil?

2. God's **Answer,** 1:5-11
   God was raising up Chaldeans to punish Judah (v. 6).

3. **2nd Problem** of the Prophet (greater than first). 1:12-17
   Why would God permit His people to be punished by a nation more wicked than they? Why did He not destroy the Chaldeans?

II. PERSPICUITY of the Prophet, ch. 2

1. **Practice** of the Prophet, 2:1
   He took the secret problem to the secret place.

2. **Patience** of the Prophet, 2:2, 3
   He waited for the vision.

3. **Pageant** for the Prophet, 2:4
   The great divide in humanity: One group, which is crooked, is flowing toward destruction; the other group, by faith, is moving toward God. This is inevitable.

4. **Parable** to the Prophet, 2:5-20
   The application is self-evident from the vision. The Chaldeans, in turn, would be destroyed. God was moving among the nations.

III. PLEASURE of the Prophet, ch. 3

1. Prayer of the Prophet, 3:1, 2

The prophet, who thought God was doing nothing about evil, now asks Him to remember to be merciful. Was he afraid that God was doing too much?

2. Program of God, 3:3-15
God rides majestically in His own chariot of salvation (v. 8).

3. Position of the Prophet, 3:16-19
He will rejoice (v. 18). He has come from pain to pleasure.

RECOMMENDED BOOKS:

(See Genesis; Hosea)

ZEPHANIAH

WRITER: Zephaniah

Zephaniah identified himself better than any of the other minor prophets. As Habakkuk concealed himself in silence, Zephaniah went to the opposite extreme and told more than is ordinary. He traced his lineage back to his great-great-grandfather, who was Hizkiah, whom we know as Hezekiah, king of Judah. He was of the royal line (1:1).

TIME:

He located the time of his writing just as clearly as he did his identification—"in the days of Josiah, the son of Amon, king of Judah" (1:1). According to the arrangement of the Hebrew Scriptures, Zephaniah was the last of the prophets before the captivity. He was contemporary with Jeremiah and probably with Micah. His was the "swan song" of the Davidic kingdom. He is credited with giving impetus to the revival during the reign of Josiah.

THEME: The dark side of love.

Sweetness and light are associated with love on every level, and rightly so, but this aspect does not exhaust the full import of love. Love expresses itself always for the good of the one who is loved. This is the reason that it is difficult to associate love with the judgment of God. The popular notion of God is that He is a super Dr. Jekyl and Mr. Hyde. One nature of His is expressed by love, and the other nature is expressed in wrath by judgment. These two appear to be contrary to the extent that there seems to be two Gods. Zephaniah is filled with the wrath and judgment of God (1:15; 3:8), but there is the undertone of the love of God (3:17). It is love which prompts a parent to take the child of the home to a hospital and to deliver him to the surgeon who endangers the life by pressing a scalpel into the vitals. This act is as much the expression of love as are the candies which are brought to the bedside the next week.

TWO THOUGHTS:

(1) "The day of the LORD" occurs 7 times. Obadiah and Joel, the first of the writing prophets, were the first to use this expression; Zephaniah, the last, brings it to our attention again. This has particular application to the great tribulation, which precedes the kingdom as well as includes it. It is a time of wrath.

(2) "Jealousy" occurs twice. It is not on the same level as human jealousy, but reveals the love of God for His people who have failed.

OUTLINE:

    I.   **Judgment** of **Judah** and **Jerusalem, ch. 1**
  II.   **Judgment** of the **Earth** and of All Nations, **2:1-3:8**
 III.   All **Judgments Removed**; Kingdom Established, **3:9-20**

RECOMMENDED BOOKS:

(See Genesis; Hosea.)

HAGGAI

Prophets to the returned remnant were Haggai, Zechariah, and Malachi.

WRITER: Haggai

Haggai is mentioned in Ezra 5:1, 2 and 6:14 as one of the two prophets who encouraged the remnant (that returned after the Babylonian captivity) to rebuild the Temple in spite of the difficulties that beset them on every hand. From this and the brief references that he made to himself in his prophecy, four things become apparent: (1) He was self-effacing—he exalted the Lord; (2) He was God's messenger—"Thus saith the LORD"; (3) He not only rebuked, he cheered and encouraged; (4) He not only preached, he practiced.

DATE: 520 B.C.

"The second year of Darius" enables the historian to pinpoint the time of this prophet in profane history. Hystaspis (the Darius mentioned here) began to reign in 521 B.C. At this same time in China, Confucius was living.

THEME: The Temple

The reconstruction and refurbishing of the Temple were the supreme passion of this prophet. He not only rebuked the people for their delay in rebuilding the Temple, but he encouraged them and helped them in this enterprise.

Haggai constantly referred to the "word of the LORD" as the supreme authority. He willingly humbled himself that the Lord might be exalted. His message was practical. It was as simple and factual as 2+2=4. The prophecy of Haggai and the epistle of James have much in common. Both put the emphasis upon the daily grind. Action is spiritual. A "do nothing" attitude is wicked. Both placed this yardstick down upon life. Work is the measure of life.

Haggai's contemporary, Zechariah, was visionary, and had his head in the clouds, but pragmatic Haggai had both feet on the ground. The man of action and the dreamer need to walk together. 1 Cor. 15:58 can appropriately be written over this book.

For the background of his message, read Ezra 3:8-13, also chapters 4, 5 and 6.

KEY VERSES: Haggai 1:8, 14

THE CALENDAR:

The compass of this book is 3 months and 14 days, according to the calendar. There are 5 messages in the book, and each was given on a specific date. The calendar furnishes the clue for the contents.

OUTLINE:

I. September 1, 520 B.C., **1:1-11**

A **CHALLENGE to the People**

1. A Charge of Conflict of Interest, 1:1-4

2. A Call to Consider Their Ways, 1:5-7

3. A Command to Construct the Temple, 1:8-11

II. September 24, 520 B.C., **1:12-15**

The **RESPONSE to the Challenge**

1. Construction of the Temple; People Obeyed, 1:12

2. Confirmation from God, 1:13, 15

III. October 21, 520 B.C., **2:1-9**

The **DISCOURAGEMENT of the People**

The **ENCOURAGEMENT of the Lord**

Haggai

(The inferiority of the 2nd Temple to the 1st Temple became a cause of discouragement, but God responded.)

IV. December 24, 520 B.C., **2:10-19**

An **APPEAL to the Law;**

The **EXPLANATION of the Principle**

V. December 24, 520 B.C., **2:20-23**

A **REVELATION of God's Program;**

An **EXPECTATION for the Future**

RECOMMENDED BOOKS:

Morgan, F. Crossley: *Haggai, a Prophet of Correction and Comfort.*

ZECHARIAH

WRITER:

Zechariah, whose name means *whom Jehovah remembers,* is identified (1:1) as the son of Berechiah, which means *Jehovah blesses,* and his father was the son of Iddo, which means *the appointed time.* Certainly this cluster of names with such rich meanings is suggestive of the encouragement given to the remnant—God remembers and blesses in the appointed time. The Jewish Targum states that Zechariah was slain in the sanctuary, and that this Zechariah was both prophet and priest. In Nehemiah 12:4 Iddo is mentioned as one of the heads of a priestly family. Josephus states that Zechariah, the son of Baruchus, was slain at the Temple. There are those who identify Zechariah as the one mentioned by our Lord as having been martyred (Matt. 23:35).

DATE: About 520 B.C.

Zechariah was contemporary with Haggai (Ezra 5:1, 6:14), although he was younger (2:4).

CHARACTERISTICS:

This book has the characteristics of an apocalypse. The visions resemble those in the books of Daniel and Revelation. Daniel was born in the land of Israel, but wrote his apocalypse outside of it. Zechariah was born outside of the land, but wrote his within the land. Daniel, Ezekiel, and John all wrote outside the land. Only Zechariah was in Israel when he wrote his apocalypse. In the dark day of discouragement which blanketed the remnant, he saw the Glory in all of the rapture and vision of hope. He has more Messianic prophecies than any of the other minor prophets.

OUTLINE:

I. **APOCALYPTIC VISIONS** (Messianic and Millennial), **chs. 1-6**

1. **Introduction** and Message of **Warning,** 1:1-6

Zechariah

   2. **Ten Visions** (all in one night), 1:7-6:15
       (1) Riders Under Myrtle Trees, 1:7-17
       (2) Four Horns, 1:18, 19
       (3) Four Smiths, 1:20, 21
       (4) Man with Measuring Line, ch. 2
       (5) Joshua and Satan, 3:1-7
       (6) The Branch, 3:8-10
       (7) Lampstand and Two Olive Trees, ch. 4
       (8) Flying Roll, 5:1-4
       (9) Woman in the Ephah, 5:5-11
      (10) Four Chariots, ch. 6

II. HISTORIC INTERLUDE, chs. 7, 8

   1. **Question** Concerning a Religious Ritual **(Fasting)**, 7:1-3

   2. Threefold **Answer**, 7:4-8:23
       (1) When the Heart is Right, the Ritual is Right, 7:4-7
       (2) When the Heart is Wrong, the Ritual is Wrong, 7:8-14
       (3) God's Purpose Concerning Jerusalem
            Unchanged by Any Ritual, ch. 8

III. PROPHETIC BURDENS, chs. 9-14

   1. First Burden: **Prophetic Aspects** Connected with
                    1st Coming of Christ, chs. 9-11

   2. Second Burden: **Prophetic Aspects** Connected with
                     2nd Coming of Christ, chs. 12-14

RECOMMENDED BOOKS:

(See Genesis; Hosea)

MALACHI

WRITER: Malachi

Malachi means "my messenger." The Septuagint gives its meaning as *angel*. An angel was a messenger, and could be either human or spiritual. There are some who conclude, therefore, that Malachi is only a title, and that the name of this prophet is not known. Surely our information of him is as limited as it is regarding the angels. Others have suggested that he was a spiritual angel, but there are no grounds for this.

The message, not the messenger, is the important issue. The Western Union boy is not as important to you as the message he delivers to you. You want his message, not his name or his visit.

DATE: Probably 397 B.C.

He concluded the prophets, as Nehemiah had concluded the historians. He prophesied either during the latter period of Nehemiah's governorship or immediately after it.

MESSAGE:

This one, who was the messenger of the Lord, delighted in using his own name when referring to other messengers. He made 3 mighty references:

(1) He referred to Levi as the messenger of the Lord (2:7). This suggests that every witness of God is an *angel* of the Lord.

(2) He announced the coming of John the Baptist as "my messenger" (3:1). John the Baptist was the Malachi of the New Testament and began where Malachi of the Old Testament left off. Malachi was the first radio announcer who said, "The next voice you will hear will be that of the Lord's messenger."

(3) He also made the definite reference to Christ as the "messenger of the covenant" (3:1). The angel of the Lord of the Old Testament is the pre-incarnate Christ.

Malachi

The method adopted by Malachi is to first quote a declaration or interrogation God makes to Israel. Then he gives Israel's answer, which is supercilious and sophisticated sarcasm. Finally, he gives God's telling reply, which is equally biting sarcasm.

Malachi's prophecy reveals an age deadened to sin. They were drugged to an unconsciousness of sin. They were in a spiritual stupor with no conviction, which is the lowest state of sin. They mouthed surprise that God would find fault. They were peevish and petulant children who affected ignorance. They pretended to know everything but were woefully lacking in a knowledge of essentials.

OUTLINE:

I. The **Love of God** for Israel, 1:1-5
II. The **Priests Reproved** for Profanity, 1:6-2:9
III. The **People Rebuked** for **Social Sins,** 2:10-17
IV. The **Prediction** of the **Two Messengers,** 3:1-6
V. The **People Rebuked** for **Religious Sins,** 3:7-18
VI. The **Prediction** of the **Day of the Lord**
   and of the **Sun of Righteousness** Who Ushers It In, ch. 4

RECOMMENDED BOOKS:

(See Genesis; Hosea.)

124

GOSPEL OF MATTTHEW

Although it is not alleged that the arrangement of the books of the Bible is inspired, it is an historical fact that spiritual and scholarly men supervised the arrangement of the books of the New Testament canon. Therefore it is no accident that the Gospel of Matthew is first. Even Renan, the French skeptic, said of this Gospel, "...the most important book in Christendom—the most important book that ever has been written." This Gospel stands like a swinging door between the two testaments. It swings back into the Old Testament and gathers up prophecies fulfilled at the first coming of Christ, and it swings into the New Testament and speaks of the "new creation" of God, "Upon this rock *I will* build my *church*" (Matt. 16:18).

WRITER: Matthew

Matthew was a converted publican (Matt. 9:9) who was chosen to write to the Jews concerning their Messiah.

KEY:

Matthew presents the program of God. The "kingdom of heaven" is an expression which is peculiar to this Gospel. It occurs 32 times. The word "kingdom" occurs 50 times. A proper understanding of the phrase "kingdom of heaven" is essential to any interpretation of the Bible. *The kingdom of heaven and the church are not the same.* John the Baptist was the first to use the expression "the kingdom of heaven" (Matt. 3:2). He began his ministry with the bold and startling announcement, "Repent ye: for the kingdom of heaven is at hand." When the Lord Jesus Christ began His ministry, He likewise began with this very announcement (Matt. 4:17). Neither John nor Jesus attempted to explain the meaning of the term. It is reasonable to assume that the people to whom the message was given had some conception of its meaning. The Jews of the first century in Palestine had a clearer understanding of the term than the average church member in Christendom today. They were not confused by the theologians of 19 centuries who have attempted to fit the term into some system of theology. In this they were fortunate. They understood the term to be the sum total of all the prophecies of the Old Testament concerning the coming of the King from heaven to set up a kingdom on this earth with heaven's standard. The concept is not new (Dan. 2:44; 7:14, 27).

"Behold Your King"

OUTLINE:

Matthew presents the Lord Jesus Christ as the King:
1. **Person** of the King, chs. 1-2
2. **Preparation** of the King, chs. 3-4:16
3. **Propaganda** of the King, chs. 4:17-9:35
4. **Program** of the King, chs. 9:36-16:20
5. **Passion** of the King, chs. 16:21-27:66
6. **Power** of the King, ch. 28

There is a movement in Matthew. Learn to think your way through the entire Gospel from the first through the twenty-eighth chapter. *You must know Matthew to understand the Bible.* You can no more understand the Bible without understanding the Gospel of Matthew than you can write without an alphabet.

Moving Through Matthew

CHAPTER

1 Genealogy and Record of Virgin Birth of Jesus

2 Visit of Wise Men—Flight to Egypt—Return to Nazareth

3 John the Baptist, Forerunner of King, Announces Kingdom and Baptizes Jesus, the King

4 Testing of the King in Wilderness—Begins Public Ministry at Capernaum—Calls Disciples

5, 6, 7 Sermon on the Mount
   (1) Relationship of Subjects of Kingdom to Self, 5:1-16
   (2) Relationship of Subjects of Kingdom to Law, 5:17-48
   (3) Relationship of Subjects of Kingdom to God, 6:1-34
   (4) Relationship of Children of King to Each Other, 7:1-29

CHAPTER

RECOMMENDED BOOKS FOR FURTHER STUDY:

Gaebelein, A. C.: *Gospel of Matthew.* Loizeaux Brothers, Inc., New York, N.Y.

Gray, James M.: *Synthetic Bible Studies.* Fleming H. Revell Co., Westwood, N.J.

Ironside, H. A.: *Gospel of Matthew.* Loizeaux Brothers, Inc., New York, N.Y.

Kelly, William: *Lectures on the Gospel of Matthew.* Loizeaux Brothers, Inc., New York, N.Y.

Moorehead, W. G.: *Studies in the Four Gospels.*

Morgan, G. Campbell: *Living Messages of the Books of the Bible,* Vol. II. Fleming H. Revell Co., Westwood, N.J.

Morgan, G. Campbell: *The Gospel According to Matthew.* Fleming H. Revell Co., Westwood, N.J.

Pettingill, W. L.: *Gospel of the Kingdom.*

Scofield, C. I.: *Bible Correspondence Course,* Vol. II.

Van Ryn, August: *Meditations in Matthew.* Loizeaux Brothers, Inc., New York, N.Y.

GOSPEL OF MARK

WRITER: Mark

John Mark—John was his Jewish name, while Mark was his Latin surname (Acts 12:12). This is the first historical reference to him in Scripture. His mother was a wealthy and prominent Christian in the Jerusalem church. He was a nephew of Barnabas (Colossians 4:10). He evidently was the spiritual son of Simon Peter (I Peter 5:13). The Gospel of Mark has long been considered Peter's gospel, as Mark evidently got much of the material of the gospel record from him. In view of the fact that Simon Peter brought him to a saving knowledge of Christ, it is natural to suppose that he had great influence in his life.

Mark joined Paul and Barnabas before the first missionary journey (Acts 13:5), but he turned back at Perga in Pamphylia (Acts 13:13). There is neither need to defend John Mark for turning back, nor to explain or excuse his conduct. It is obvious that he failed in the eyes of Paul. Paul's refusal to permit him to accompany them on the second missionary journey is witness enough (Acts 15:37, 38). It severed the combination of Paul and Barnabas (Acts 15:39). Let us hasten to assure you that John Mark made good later on, even Paul acknowledged him as a profitable servant of the Lord (2 Timothy 4:11). (Also note another reference made by Paul to Mark in Philemon 24.)

DATE:

Since this was the earliest of the Gospels written, the date of its writing was probably prior to A.D. 63. It is quite likely that it was written from Rome to the Romans. No doubt Mark was with Paul in Rome at the time. The Epistle of Paul to the Romans had preceded him and was in circulation there.

THEME:

There are two phrases in the first chapter which set before the reader the theme of this Gospel:

"The beginning of the Gospel of Jesus Christ"—Verse 1

"Jesus came"—verses 9 and 14

Mark presents the beginning of the Gospel. It is not the beginning of Jesus Christ, but the beginning of the Gospel.

"JESUS CAME"—Mark roots this phrase in the prophecy of Isaiah and the proclamation of John the Baptist, and not in Bethlehem or in Jerusalem as we find in John's Gospel. He begins with Jesus at His baptism, temptation and His ministry in Galilee. Mark is the Gospel of miracles. Jesus is presented as the Servant of Jehovah (Isaiah 42:1, 2).

Jesus came in the winsomeness of His humanity and the fulness of His deity doing good. This was only the beginning of the Gospel. He died and rose again. Then He said to His own, "Go." The Gospel was then completed. This is the Gospel today.

KEY VERSE: Mark 10:45

PECULIAR CHARACTERISTICS:

The style of Mark is brief and blunt, pertinent and pithy, short and sweet. Mark is stripped of excess verbiage and goes right to the point. This is the Gospel of action and accomplishment. Here Jesus is not adorned with words and narrative but He is stripped and girded for action.

Mark is written in a simple style. It is designed for the mass of the street. It is interesting to note that the connective *and* occurs more than any other word in the Gospel. It occurs 1,331 times. It will reward the reader to thumb through the Gospel and note the chapters and verses where this is true. Modern rhetoric might consider that a breach of good grammar, yet there is no word that conveys action as does this word.

Mark wrote this Gospel in Rome, evidently for Romans. They were a busy people and believed in power and action. This Gospel was brief enough for a busy man to read and would appeal to the Roman mind. Few Old Testament Scriptures are quoted and Jewish customs explained which gives additional proof that it was written for foreigners.

Mark

OUTLINE:

The Credentials of Christ

I. John INTRODUCES the Servant, 1:1-8
(Death of John, 6:14-29)
II. God the Father IDENTIFIES the Servant, 1:9-11
(9:1-8, Transfiguration)
III. The Temptation INITIATES the Servant, 1:12, 13
IV. Works and Words ILLUSTRATE (Illumine)
the Servant, 1:14-13:37

1. Miracles

(1) *Healing (Physical)*
(a) Peter's Wife's Mother (fever), and Others, 1:29-34
(b) Leper, 1:40-45
(c) Palsied Man Let Down Through Roof, 2:1-12
(d) Man with Withered Hand, 3:1-5
(e) Many Healed by Sea of Galilee, 3:6-10
(f) Woman with Issue of Blood, 5:21-34
(g) Sick at Nazareth, 6:5
(h) Disciples Heal, 6:13
(i) Sick in Land of Gennesaret, 6:53-56
(j) Deaf and Dumb of Decapolis, 7:31-37
(k) Blind Man of Bethsaida, 8:22-26
(l) Blind Bartimaeus, 10:46-52
(2) *Nature (Natural)*
(a) Stills the Storm, 4:35-41
(b) Five Thousand Fed, 6:32-44
(c) Walks on Sea, 6:45-52
(d) Four Thousand Fed, 8:1-9
(e) Fig Tree Cursed, 11:12-14
(3) *Demons (Spiritual)*
(a) Man in Synagogue, 1:21-27
(b) Many Demons in Capernaum, 1:32-34
(c) Demons in Galilee, 1:39
(d) Unclean Spirits by Sea of Galilee, 3:11, 12
(e) Scribes Charge that
He Casts Out Demons by Beelzebub, 3:22-30
(4) *Raised from Dead (Supernatural)*
Daughter of Jairus, 5:35-43

132

2. Parables and Teaching

(1) *Parables*
    (a) Fasting with the Bridegroom Present, 2:19, 20
    (b) New Cloth on Old Garment, 2:21
    (c) New Wine in Old Bottles, 2:22
    (d) Sower, 4:1-20
    (e) Candle and Bushel, 4:21-25
    (f) Seed Growing, 4:26-29
    (g) Mustard Seed, 4:30-34
    (h) Man Demanding Fruit from Vineyard, 12:1-12
    (i) Fig Tree, 13:28-33
    (j) Man on Trip, 13:34-37

(2) *Miscellaneous Teachings*
    (a) Preaching the Gospel of the Kingdom, 1:14, 15
    (b) Preaching in Galilee, 1:28, 35-39
    (c) Sabbath, 2:23-28
    (d) New Relationship, 3:31-35
    (e) Synagogue in Nazareth, 6:1-6
    (f) The Twelve Sent Out, 6:7-13
    (g) The Twelve Return, 6:30-31
    (h) Pharisees Denounced, 7:1-23
    (i) Leaven Explained, 8:10-21
    (j) Death of Christ, 8:27-38; 9:30-32; 10:32-34
    (k) Mark of Greatness, 9:33-37
    (l) Rebuke of Sectarianism, 9:38-41
    (m) Hell, 9:42-50
    (n) Marriage, 10:1-16
    (o) Riches, 10:23-31
    (p) Prayer, 11:22-26
    (q) Authority of Jesus, 11:27-33
    (r) Taxes, 12:13-17
    (s) Resurrection, 12:18-27
    (t) The Great Commandment, 12:28-34
    (u) Messiah, 12:35-40
    (v) Olivet Discourse, 13:1-27

(3) *Incidents*
    (a) Call of Disciples, 1:16-20; 2:13-18; 3:13-21
    (b) Death of John the Baptist, 6:14-29
    (c) Transfiguration, 9:1-13
    (d) Rich Young Ruler, 10:17-22
    (e) Ambition of James and John, 10:35-45

    (f) Triumphal Entry, 11:1-11
    (g) Jesus Cleanses Temple, 11:15-18
    (h) Fig Tree Withered, 11:19-21
    (i) Widow's Mite, 12:41-44

V. Death, Burial and Resurrection
INSURE the Servant. 14:1–16:20

1. Plot to Put Jesus to Death, 14:1, 2
2. Jesus at Supper in Bethany, 14:3-9
3. Judas Bargains to Betray Jesus, 14:10-11
4. The Passover, 14:12-26
5. The Garden of Gethsemane, 14:27-42
6. The Arrest of Jesus, 14:43-52
7. The Trial of Jesus, 14:53-15:15
8. The Crucifixion of Jesus, 15:16-41
9. The Burial, 15:42-47
10. The Resurrection, 16:1-20

RECOMMENDED BOOKS FOR FURTHER STUDY:

English, E. S.: *Studies in the Gospel According to Mark.*
Erdman, Charles R.: *The Gospel of Mark.*
Ironside, H. A.: *Mark.*
McGee, J. Vernon: *Marching Through Mark.*
Morgan, G. Campbell: *The Gospel According to Mark.*

GOSPEL OF LUKE

WRITER: Luke

Luke was the "beloved physician" of Colossians 4:14. He used more medical terms than Hippocrates, the father of medicine. The choice of Luke by the Holy Spirit to write the third Gospel reveals that there are no accidental writers of Scripture. There was a supernatural selection of Luke. There were "not many wise" called, but Luke belongs to that category. He and Paul were evidently on a very high intellectual level as well as a spiritual level. This explains partially why they traveled together and obviously became fast friends in the Lord.

Dr. Luke would rank as a scientist of his day. He wrote the best Greek of any of the New Testament writers including Paul. He was an accurate historian. According to Sir William Ramsay, Dr. Luke was a careful historian of remarkable ability.

A great deal of tradition surrounds the life of Dr. Luke which is needless for us to examine in a brief analysis. He writes his Gospel from Mary's viewpoint, which confirms the tradition that he got his information for his Gospel from her. Surely he conferred with her. Also there is every reason to believe that he was a Gentile. Most scholars concur in this position. Paul, in Colossians, distinguishes between those "who are of the circumcision" (Col. 4:11) and the others who are obviously Gentiles. Luke is in the list of Gentiles (Col. 4:14). (Sir William Ramsay and J. M. Stifler affirm without reservation that Luke was a Gentile.)

References to Luke: Col. 4:14; 2 Tim. 4:11; Philemon 24; also the "we" section of Acts—Acts 16:10-17; 20:5 - 21:18; 27:1 - 28:16.

THEME: "Behold the Man"

Jesus is the *second* man, but the *last* Adam (1 Cor. 15:45, 47). He is making men like Jesus (1 John 3:2), therefore Jesus is the *second* man—for there will be the third and even the millionth. He is the *last* Adam, as there will *not* be another head of the human family. Jesus was "made like unto His brethern" (Heb. 2:17) that His brethern might be made like unto Him.

THE SCIENTIFIC APPROACH:

Matthew emphasizes that Jesus was born the Messiah. Mark emphasizes that Jesus was the Servant of Jehovah. Luke stresses the fact that Jesus was the perfect Man. John presents the fact that God became a Man, but that is not the scientific approach.

Dr. Luke states that he examined Jesus of Nazareth, and his findings are that Jesus is God. He came to the same conclusion as John, but his procedure and technique were different.

SPECIAL FEATURES:

1. Although the Gospel of Luke is one of the synoptic Gospels, it contains many features omitted by Matthew and Mark.
2. Dr. Luke gives us the songs of Christmas.
3. Dr. Luke has the longest account of the virgin birth of Jesus of any of the Gospels. In the first two chapters he gives us an unabashed record of obstetrics. A clear and candid statement of the virgin birth is given by Dr. Luke. All the way from Dr. Luke to Dr. Howard Kelly, gynecologist of John Hopkins, there is a mighty affirmation of the virgin birth, which makes the statements of pseudo-theologians seem rather puerile when they unblushingly state that the virgin birth is a biological impossibility.
4. Dr. Luke gives us 20 miracles and 6 of them are recorded in no other Gospel.
5. He likewise gives us 23 parables and 18 of them are found nowhere else. The parables of the Prodigal Son and the Good Samaritan are peculiar to the third Gospel.
6. He also gives us the very human account of the walk to Emmaus of our resurrected Lord. This proves that Jesus was still human after His resurrection. Dr. Luke demonstrates that the resurrection was not of the spirit but of the body. Jesus was "sown a natural body...raised a spiritual *body*."
7. A definite human sympathy pervades this Gospel, which reveals the truly human nature of Jesus, as well as the bighearted sympathy of this physician of the first century who knew first hand a great deal about the suffering of humanity.

8. Dr. Luke uses more medical terms than Hippocrates, the father of medicine.

OUTLINE:

I. Birth of the Perfect Man and His Family, chs. 1-3

1. Events Connected with Birth of John the Baptist; Announcement of Gabriel to Mary, ch. 1

2. Events Connected with Birth of Jesus; Incident from Boyhood of Jesus, ch. 2

3. Message of John the Baptist; Genealogy of Mary, ch. 3

II. Testing of the Perfect Man; His Home Town, ch. 4

1. Temptation of Jesus, 4:1-13

2. Rejection by Nazareth, His Home Town, 4:14-30

3. Moves His Headquarters to Capernaum, 4:31-48

III. Ministry of the Perfect Man, chs. 5-21

1. Jesus Calls His Apostles; Heals and Teaches Around Sea of Galilee, **ch. 5**

2. Jesus Heals on Sabbath; Chooses Apostles; Teaches on the Plain, **ch. 6**

3. Jesus Heals and Raises Dead; Commends John the Baptist; Goes to Dinner in Home of Pharisee, **ch. 7**

4. Jesus Teaches and Heals Around Sea of Galilee; Crosses Gadara and Returns, **ch. 8**

5. Jesus Sends Apostles to Preach and Heal; Hears Their Confession; Announces His Death and Resurrection; is Transfigured; Begins His March to Jerusalem, **ch. 9**

6. Jesus Sends Forth the 70; Pronounces Judgment on Cities

2. Jesus Taken to Pilate, Sent Before Herod; Returned to Pilate; Condemned to Take Barabbas' Place; Crucified and Buried, **ch. 23**

V. Resurrection of the Perfect Man, ch. 24

Resurrection of Jesus, Jesus Walks Emmaus Road; Appears to 10; Commissions Disciples; Ascends to Heaven, **ch. 24**

RECOMMENDED BOOKS FOR FURTHER STUDY:

Erdman, Charles R.: *The Gospel of Luke.*
Ironside, H. A.: *Addresses on the Gospel of Luke.*
Morgan, G. Campbell: *The Gospel According to Luke.*
Stifler, James M.: *The Christ of Christianity.*

GOSPEL OF JOHN

WRITER: John

John was an apostle, son of Zebedee and Salome, and brother of James (Mark 1:19, 20 ; Matt. 20:20; John 21:20-24). His authorship has been seriously questioned by the Tubingen school of critics; however, the objections have been fully answered by the Dead Sea scrolls and also by the dating of carbon 14, and the Johannean authorship is received by competent Bible scholarship.

It is interesting to note that the following early church fathers ascribe the fourth Gospel to John: Theophilus, Bishop of Antioch —A.D. 180; Iraneaus—A.D. 190, pupil of Polycarp, who in turn was pupil of John; Clement of Alexandria—A.D. 200; and the Muratorium fragment says the fourth Gospel is by John.

DATE:

A.D. 90-100. Some suppose that this is the last book of the New Testament to be written. However, it seems appropriate to consider the writings of John in sequence: namely, Gospel of John, the three Epistles, and the Revelation. All were written evidently during the last ten years of the life of the "beloved apostle."

STRUCTURE:

There are several striking features about the structure:

1. The first 3 Gospels are called the synoptic Gospels because they are written from the same viewpoint. The fourth Gospel is different.

(a) Matthew and Mark emphasize the miracles of Jesus, and Luke gives attention to the parables; John does neither.

(b) The miracles in John are given as signs, and were chosen with a great deal of discrimination in order to interpret certain great truths (*e.g.,* Jesus fed the 5000, and follows it with His discourse on the Bread of Life).

There are eleven specific signs in John.

(c) There are no parables in the fourth Gospel. The word *parable* occurs one time (10:6), but is not the regular Greek word *parabole* but *paroimia*. The story of the Good Shepherd is not a parable but a discourse. The record of the lost sheep in Luke 15 is a parable. In John the figures which Jesus used are in the nature of metaphors.

2. The simplicity of language has caused some to label John's record as the "simple" Gospel. The fact that so many monosyllabic and disyllabic words occur has deceived many. This is the most profound Gospel, and the most difficult to fathom its meaning. Consider this simple statement and then try to probe its depths,—"and ye in me, and I in you" (John 14:20).

3. John gives a chronological order which is well to note (*e.g.*, "the next day," 1:29, 35, 43). He presents a logical and chronological sequence. He also gives attention to places and cities (*e.g.*, "Bethabara, beyond Jordan," 1:28; "Cana of Galilee," 2:1).

4. Although the deity of Christ is in the foreground, the humanity of Christ is not lost sight of but is peculiarly emphasized (*e.g.*, "Jesus...being wearied with his journey,"4:6).

5. The name *Jesus* is used almost entirely to the exclusion of *Christ*. This seems strange in the Gospel which sets forth His deity.

6. The word *Jew* occurs over 60 times.

WHY JOHN WROTE:

Several explanations have been offered as the reasons John wrote his Gospel:

1. To correct the synoptic Gospels (invalid since he did not deal with their material);

2. To correct wrong view concerning John the Baptist;

3. To refute errors of Cerinthus;

4. John's own reason—John 20:30, 31.

ESTIMATION:

During the entire life of the church there have been many glowing tributes paid to the fourth Gospel. Some have called this "the heart of Christ," the "spiritual Gospel," and in Europe it is called "the bosom of Christ."

Origen said, "The Gospel is the consummation of the Gospels as the Gospels are of the Scriptures."

Jerome said, "John excels in the depths of divine mysteries."

Culross: "I believe the writings of John have been blotted by more penitents' tears and have won more hearts for the Redeemer, than all the rest put together."

A. T. Pierson: "It touches the heart of Christ. If Matthew corresponds to the court of Israel, Mark to the court of the Priests, and Luke to the court of the Gentiles, John leads us past the veil into the Holy of Holies."

D. A. Hayes: "As we read we are assured that here at last is the worthy and adequate picture of the life of Jesus among men."

THEME:

The deity of Jesus is the paramount purpose. The Messianic character also holds priority. This is succinctly stated in John 20:31.

There is a mighty movement which is stated in John 16:28. God became a man; this is the simple statement of the sublime fact. John Wesley expressed it, "God contracted to a span."

These things are recorded to beget faith in the heart of man. *Believe* is used over 100 times in John's Gospel. It occurs less than 40 times in the synoptic Gospels. The noun *faith* does not occur in John, but is used in the other Gospels. *Eternal life* occurs 35 times, but only 12 times in the synoptic Gospels.

OUTLINE:

I. Prologue—Incarnation, **1:1-18**
Word is God (vv. 1-3)
Word became Flesh (v. 14)
Word Revealed God (v. 18)

II. Introduction, 1:19-51

1. Witness of John the Baptist, 1:19-36
Jesus is Revealer of God (v. 36); Redeemer of Man (v. 29)
2. Witness of Andrew, 1:37-42
Jesus is the Messiah (Christ)(v. 41)
3. Witness of Philip, 1:43-46
Jesus Fulfillment of Old Testament (v. 45)
4. Witness of Nathanael, 1:47-51
Jesus is Son of God, King of Israel (v. 49)

III. Witness of Works and Words ("Signs" 20:30, 31), **chs. 2-12**

1. Jesus at Marriage in Cana (1st Work), **2**:1-12
2. Jesus Cleanses Temple During Passover in Jerusalem (1st Word), 2:13-22
Jesus is Resurrection (v. 22)
3. Jesus Interviews Nicodemus
in Jerusalem (2nd Word), 2:23-**3**:36
Jesus Must Die for Sins of World (3:15)
4. Jesus Interviews Woman at Well in Sychar (3rd Word), **4**:1-45
Jesus is Giver of Water of Life
5. Jesus Heals Nobleman's Son
in Capernaum (2nd Work), 4:46-54
6. Jesus Heals Man at Pool of Bethesda (3rd Work), **ch. 5**
Jesus is Equal with God
7. Jesus Feeds 5.000
on East of Sea of Galilee (4th Work & Word), **ch. 6**
Jesus is Bread of Life
8. Jesus Teaches at Feast of Tabernacle
in Temple (5th Word), **ch. 7**
Jesus is Water of Life; Promises the Holy Spirit

    e. Trial before Pilate, vv. 38-40
2. Death of Jesus at Golgotha; Burial in Tomb of Joseph, **ch. 19**
3. Resurrection of Jesus; Appearances to Mary, Disciples, Thomas, **ch. 20**

VI. Epilogue—Glorification, **ch. 21**

The Resurrected Jesus Is Still God
Lord of Our Wills—Directs our Service (v. 6)
Lord of Our Hearts—Motive for Service (vv. 15-17)
Lord of Our Minds—Lack of Knowledge No Excuse from Service (v. 22)

Another division of the Gospel of John:
    John 1-12 LIGHT
    John 13-17 LOVE
    John 18-21 LIFE

RECOMMENDED BOOKS:

Erdman, Charles R.: *The Gospel of John.*
Ironside, Harry A.: *Addresses on the Gospel of John.*
Lee, Robert: *The Outlined John.*
Meyer, F. B.: *The Life and Light of Men* also *Love to the Uttermost.*
Morgan, G. Campbell: *Gospel of John.*
Ryle, J. C.: *Expository Thoughts on the Gospels.*

ACTS

(Sometimes called the 5th Gospel, it is a continuation of the Gospel of Luke.)

Last recorded fact about Jesus in the Gospels:

Matthew	—Resurrection	Acts 1
Mark	—Ascension	brings
Luke	—Promise of the Holy Spirit	all 4
John	—Promise of the Second Coming	together

Great missionary commission, given in the 4 Gospels, is confirmed in Acts.

Acts furnishes a ladder on which to place the Epistles.

Acts is a bridge between the Gospels and the Epistles.

The New Testament without Acts leaves a great yawning gap. "If the book of Acts were gone, there would be nothing to replace it."—Howson.

WRITER: Dr. Luke, who also wrote the third Gospel (Acts 1:1).

Sir William Ramsay says that Luke is the greatest of all historians, ancient or modern *(The Church in the Roman Empire; St. Paul, the Traveler and Roman Citizen)*.

DATE: About A.D. 63

Acts covers a period of approximately 30 years. This is the inspired record of the beginnings of the Church. While Genesis records the origin of the physical universe, Acts records the origin of the spiritual body.

KEY VERSE: Acts 1:8

SPECIAL FEATURES:

1. Prominence of the Lord Jesus Christ.

2. Prominence of the Holy Spirit
   Christ promised to send the Holy Spirit (John 7:37-39; John 14:16, 17; John 20:22; Acts 1:8). This is the age of the Holy Spirit. The great fact of this age is the indwelling of the Holy Spirit (1 Cor. 6:19).

3. Power of the Church.

4. Prominence of the Church, visible and invisible (a new institution).

5. Prominence of places—begins in Jerusalem, ends in Rome. (Ramsay checked the many places referred to.)

6. Prominence of persons—Dr. Luke mentions 110 persons by name.

7. Prominence of the resurrection, the center of Gospel preaching.

8. Prominence of Peter in the first section, and Paul in the last section (there is a strange omission of the other apostles).

TITLE:

The proper title for this historical book is the supreme problem.
   "The Acts of the Apostles"—Authorized and Revised Versions
   "The Acts of the Apostles"—Codex Vaticanus (MSS)
   "The Acts of the Ascended and Glorified Lord"—Robert Lee
   "Words Concerning Deeds"—Bantu title

Acts 1:1, 2 gives the key to the problem:
   "The Lord Jesus Christ at work by the Holy Spirit through the Apostles" (human instrumentalities).

OUTLINE:

I. **The Lord Jesus Christ at Work By the Holy Spirit Through the APOSTLES in JERUSALEM, chs. 1-7**

1. **Preparation** for the Coming of the Spirit, **ch. 1**
   (1) Introduction, vv. 1, 2

(2) 40 Days Post-Resurrection Ministry of Jesus, vv. 3-9
(3) Ascension and Promise of the Return of Jesus, vv. 10, 11
(4) Waiting for the Spirit, vv. 12-14
(5) Appointment of an Apostle, vv. 15-26

2. Day of **Pentecost** (Bethlehem of the Holy Spirit), **ch. 2**
(1) Coming of the Holy Spirit, vv. 1-13
(2) 1st Sermon in the Church Age by Peter, vv. 14-47

3. 1st **Miracle** of the Church; Peter's 2nd **Sermon, ch. 3**
(1) Healing of Lame Man, vv. 1-11
(2) Appealing and Revealing Address of Peter, vv. 12-26
(3) Believing 5000 Men (Results)—4:4

4. 1st **Persecution** of the Church; Power of the Holy Spirit, **ch. 4**

5. Death of **Ananias** and **Sapphira**; 2nd Persecution, **ch. 5**
(Discipline within and persecution without)
6. Appointment of Deacons; Witness of **Stephen,** a Deacon, **ch. 6**

7. Stephen's Address and Martyrdom (1st Martyr), **ch. 7**

II. **The Lord Jesus Christ at Work By the Holy Spirit Through the APOSTLES in JUDEA and SAMARIA, chs. 8-12**

1. Conversion of **Ethiopian** Eunuch (Son of Ham), **ch. 8**

2. Conversion of **Saul** of Tarsus (Son of Shem), **ch. 9**

3. Conversion of **Cornelius,**
Roman Centurion (Son of Japheth), **ch. 10**

4. Peter Defends His Ministry; Gospel Goes to Antioch, **ch. 11**

5. Death of James; Arrest of **Peter, ch. 12**

III. **The Lord Jesus Christ at Work By the Holy Spirit Through the APOSTLES to the UTTERMOST Part of the EARTH, chs. 13-28**

1. **1st Missionary Journey** of Paul, **chs. 13, 14**

2. Council at Jerusalem, **ch. 15**

3. **2nd Missionary Journey** of Paul 15:36-ch. **16**

4. 2nd Missionary Journey (continued)
   Paul in Thessalonica, Athens, **ch. 17**

5. 2nd Missionary Journey (continued)
   Paul in Corinth; Apollos in Ephesus, **ch. 18**

6. 2nd Missionary Journey (continued)
   Paul in Ephesus, **ch. 19**

7. **3rd Missionary Journey** of Paul, **ch. 20**

8. Paul Goes to Jerusalem and is **Arrested, ch. 21**

9. Paul's Defense before the **Mob** at Jerusalem, **ch. 22**

10. Paul's Defense before the **Sanhedrin, ch. 23**

11. Paul before **Felix, ch. 24**

12. Paul before **Festus, ch. 25**

13. Paul before **Agrippa, ch. 26**

14. Paul Goes to Rome via Storm and **Shipwreck, ch. 27**

15. Paul Arrives in **Rome, ch. 28**
    (Last seen preaching to Gentiles)

RECOMMENDED BOOKS:

Erdman, Charles R.: *The Acts.*
Gaebelein, A. C.: *The Acts of the Apostles.*
Lenski, R. C. H.: *Interpretation of the Acts of the Apostles.*
Morgan, G. Campbell: *The Acts of the Apostles.*
Stifler, James M.: *The Christ of Christianity.*
Stifler, James M.: *Introduction to the Book of Acts.*
Thomas, W. H. Griffith: *Acts of the Apostles.*

ROMANS

WRITER: Paul

DATE: A.D. 57-58

PLACE: Corinth

This Epistle was written during Paul's 3rd missionary journey, at Corinth where he spent 3 months (January to March, A.D. 57). He had just come from Ephesus where he had spent 3 strenuous years.

OCCASION:

This letter was brought forth by natural reason. Paul wished to visit Rome on his way to Spain. The letter was taken by Phoebe, deaconess of Cenchrea (16:1).

SUBJECT: The righteousness of God

Romans contains the great Gospel manifesto for the world. To Paul the Gospel was the great ecumenical movement, and Rome was the center of that world for which Christ died. Romans is an eloquent and passionate declaration of the Gospel of Jesus Christ by a man who made an arduous but productive journey to die for Christ—the One who died for him. Romans is more than cold logic; it is the Gospel stated in warm love.

KEY VERSES: Rom. 1:16, 17

ESTIMATION:

The reading of Romans is one of the most rewarding experiences in the life of a Christian. This is not to say that it should be read as a magazine article which is put aside and dismissed from the mind. It is the continual reading of this Epistle which brings a stream of benefits to the believer. The investment of a great amount of time pays handsome dividends on the spiritual market. Griffith Thomas wrote, "The Epistle should be studied with all possible intellectual attention and concentration....It is important that the whole Epistle should be read right through in the Revised Version at one sitting, and that this should be done, if possible, day by day for a month....the advantage will soon be immense. It should be studied with earnest prayer and personal trust. Intellectual attention alone is insufficient. The Epistle should be regarded as a personal letter to ourselves."

Romans requires all the mental make-up we have and then it must be bathed in prayer and supplication before the Holy Spirit can teach us.

This Epistle is the greatest document on our salvation! William Newell says that Romans is the Gospel. Every Christian should make an effort to know Romans, for this book will ground the believer in the faith.

Read Romans Regularly—Really Read Romans

These 3 features will become dominant in the life of one who constantly reads Romans:

UNDERSTANDING of the basic facts of salvation;
UNUSUAL CONVICTION about matters pertaining to the faith;
USEFULNESS in practical Christian service.

OUTLINE (in brief):

1.	Salutation	1:1-17
2.	Sin	1:18-3:20
3.	Salvation	3:21-5:10
4.	Sanctification	5:11-6:23
5.	Struggle	7
6.	Spirit-filled Living	8:1-27
7.	Security	8:28-39
8.	Segregation	9-11
9.	Sacrifice & Service	12-13
10.	Separation	14-15
11.	Salutation	16

Romans

OUTLINE:

I. DOCTRINAL, chs. 1-8 "Faith"

1. Justification of the Sinner 1:1-5:11

A. Introduction 1:1-17
(1) Paul's Personal Greeting 1:1-7
(2) Paul's Personal Purpose 1:8-13
(3) Paul's Three "I Am's" 1:14-17
(Key verses 16, 17—the revelation of the righteousness of God)

B. Revelation of the Sin of Man 1:18-3:20

This is "Sinnerama."
Universal fact: Man is a sinner.
Ecumenical Movement is away from God.
Axiom: World is guilty before God—all need righteousness.

(1) Revelation of the Wrath of God Against Sin of Man 1:18-32
  (a) Natural Revelation of God (Original Version) 1:18-20
  (b) Sub-natural Response of Man (Reversion) 1:21-23
  (c) Unnatural Retrogression of Man (Perversion) 1:24-27
  (d) Supernatural Requital of God (Inversion) 1:28-32
(2) Revelation of the Sin of Good People 2:1-16
  (Respectable people need righteousness.)
(3) Revelation of the Sin of Israel under Law 2:17-3:8
(4) Revelation of the Universality of Sin 3:9-20
  (a) Judge's Verdict of Guilty against Mankind 3:9-12
    (Man cannot remove guilt.)
  (b) Great Physician's Diagnosis of Mankind 3:13-18
    (Man cannot change his nature. Man has incurable disease.)
  (c) Purpose of the Law 3:19-20
    (Law reveals sin not salvation. Last word "sin" 3:20).

C. Revelation of the Righteousness of God 3:21-5:11

Righteousness Provided
(Righteousness of God defined—not the character of God

nor self-righteousness of man)
(1) Justification by Faith *Explained* 3:21-31

DEFINITION: Justification is the act of God that declares a sinner righteous by faith on the merit of Christ's sacrifice. It is the addition of the righteousness of Christ as well as the subtraction of sins.
> *Propitiation—"mercy seat" (Hebrews 9:5)*
> *Redemption—to pay a price for deliverance*
> *Propitiation is toward God*
> *Redemption is toward sin*

(2) Justification by Faith *Illustrated* 4:1-25
  (Demonstration—Abraham and David)
(3) Justification by Faith—*Results Derived* 5:1-11

Eight benefits:
(a) Peace—v. 1 .
(b) Access—v. 2
(c) Hope—v. 2
(d) Patience—fruit of tribulations—v. 3
(e) Love—v. 5
(f) Holy Spirit—v. 5
(g) Deliverance from the Great Tribulation—v. 9
(h) Joy—v. 11
> *Reconciliation is toward man. Definition: Change from enmity to friendship. Justification by faith is an act of God which is permanent.*

2. Sanctification of the Saint 5:12-8:39

A. Potential Sanctification 5:12-21
Federal Headship of Adam and Christ
(1) Headship of Adam 5:12-14
  Death—Sin
(2) Headship of Christ 5:15-17
  Life—Righteousness
(3) Offense of Adam vs. Righteousness of Christ 5:18-21
  Disobedience   vs. Obedience
  Judgment   vs. Free Gift
  Sin   vs. Grace
  Condemnation   vs. Justification

B. Positional Sanctification 6:1-10
Union with Christ in His death and resurrection the basis of deliverance from sin.

C. Practical Sanctification 6:11-23
Obedience to God leads to the experience of deliverance from sin.

D. Powerless Sanctification 7:1-25

(1) Shackles of a Saved Soul 7:1-14
Spiritual Emancipation
(2) Struggle of a Saved Soul 7:15-25
Civil War *(No good in old nature, no power in new nature)*

E. God's New Provision for Sanctification 8:1-39
(Powerful Sanctification)

(1) New Law: Holy Spirit vs. Law 8:1-4
(2) New Struggle: Holy Spirit vs. Flesh 8:5-13
(3) New Man, Son of God:
Holy Spirit and Spirit of Man 8:14-17
(4) New Creation: Old vs. New, Bondage vs. Liberty 8:18-22
(5) New Body: Groaning vs. Redeemed Body 8:23-27
(Holy Spirit helps us in our present bodies.)
(6) New Purpose of God 8:28-34
(God's purpose guarantees the Salvation of sinners.)
(7) New Security of the Believer 8:35-39
(God's love guarantees the Security of the believer.)

II. DISPENSATIONAL, chs. 9-11 "Hope"

1. God's Past Dealings with Israel, ch. 9
A. Israel Defined 9:1-5
B. Israel Identified 9:6-13
C. Choice of Israel in the Sovereign Purpose of God 9:14-24
D. Choice of Gentiles
in the Scriptural Prophecies of God 9:25-33

2. God's Present Purpose with Israel, ch. 10

A. Present State of Israel—Lost 10:1-4
   (Reason: Christ is the end of the law for righteousness.)
B. Present Standing of Israel—Same as Gentiles 10:5-12
   ("For there is no difference")
C. Present Salvation for Both Jew and Gentile—Hear and Believe the Gospel 10:13-21

3. **God's Future Purpose with Israel**—Remnant Regathered as a Nation and Redeemed, **ch. 11**

   A. Remnant of Israel Finding Salvation 11:1-6
   B. Remainder of Israel Blinded 11:7-12
   C. Reason for Setting Aside the Nation Israel—Salvation of the Gentiles 11:13-21
   D. Restoration of Nation Israel—Greater Blessing 11:22-32
   E. Reason for Restoring the Nation Israel 11:33-36
      (Locked in the riches of the wisdom of God)

III. DUTY, chs. 12-16 "Love"

1. **Service of "the sons of God" chs. 12-13**

   A. Relationship to God *("Present—Yield")* 12:1-2
   B. Relationship to Gifts of the Spirit 12:3-8
   C. Relationship to Other Believers 12:9-16
   D. Relationship to Unbelievers 12:17-21
   E. Relationship to Government 13:1-7
   F. Relationship to Neighbors 13:8-14

2. **Separation of "the Sons of God" chs. 14-16**

   A. Relationship to Weak Believers 14:1-15:3
      Three Principles of Conduct for Christians
      (1) Conviction 14:5
      (2) Conscience 14:22
      (3) Consideration 15:1-2
   B. Relationship of Jews and Gentiles as Believers 15:4-13
      (Racial Relationships)
   C. Relationship of Paul
      to Romans and Gentiles Generally 15:14-33
      (The Gospel and Gentiles 15:16)

Romans

    D. Relationship of Christians
       to One Another Demonstrated 16:1-27
       *(Thirty-five persons mentioned by name—mutual love and
       tender affection.)*

RECOMMENDED BOOKS:

Harrison, Norman B.: *His Salvation.*
Ironside, H. A.: *Lectures on the Epistle to the Romans.*
McGee, J. Vernon: *Reasoning Through Romans,* Vols. 1 & 2.
Newell, William R.: *Romans.*
Thomas, W. H. Griffith: *St. Paul's Epistle to the Romans.*

I & II CORINTHIANS

WRITER: Paul

DATE: A.D. 55-57 (More likely 57)

PLACE: Written from Ephesus

THEME: The Lordship of Jesus (I Cor. 1:2, 3, 7-10)

BACKGROUND:

Carnal Corinth was the sin center of the Roman Empire in Paul's day. It was labeled "Vanity Fair." Its location was about 40 miles west of Athens on a narrow isthmus between Peloponnesus and the mainland. It was the great commercial center of the Roman Empire with 3 harbors, of which two were important— Lechaeum, about 1½ miles to the west, and Cenchrea, about 8½ miles to the east.

196 B.C. Rome declared it a free city.
146 B.C. It rebelled and was totally destroyed by Mummius, the consul.
46 B.C.   Julius Caesar rebuilt the city in great elegance, restoring it to its former prominence.

However, even its ruins were lost to history for many years, and a fishing village was built over them. In 1928 an earthquake uncovered them, and now much of the city has been excavated.

The temple of Aphrodite, built on the Acrocorinthus, was attended by 1,000 priestesses of vice, actually nothing more than prostitutes.

The city was given over to licentiousness and pleasure. The Isthmian games were conducted here.

Against this corrupt background, Paul preached the Gospel in Corinth, founded the church, and wrote two epistles, I and II Corinthians.

Read Acts 18:1-18 for the account of Paul's visit to Corinth.

I CORINTHIANS

I Corinthians is obviously Paul's answer to a previous letter which he had written to the Corinthians (1 Cor. 5:9). They sent a delegation with a letter (1 Cor. 7:1; 16:17) and I Corinthians is Paul's reply concerning the conditions in the Corinthian church. It is a letter of errors and confirmation of truth.

OUTLINE:

I. **Salutation and Thanksgiving, 1:1-9**

II. **Concerning Conditions in the Corinthian Church, 1:10-16:9**

1. Concerning **DIVISIONS** and Party Spirit, 1:10-4:21

 (1) **Centrality** of Christ Crucified
 Corrects Divisions, 1:10-31

 (2) **Clarity** of Holy Spirit
 Corrects Human Wisdom, ch. 2

 (3) **Correct Conception** of God
 Clarifies Christian Service, ch. 3

 (4) **Conditions** of Christ's Servants
 Constrain Christian Conduct, ch. 4

2. Concerning **SCANDALS** in the Corinthian Church, 5:1-6:20

 (1) Impurity, 5:1-13
 (2) Lawsuits among Members, ch. 6

3. Concerning **MARRIAGE,** ch. 7

4. Concerning **CHRISTIAN LIBERTY,** 8:1-11:1

5. Concerning **WOMAN'S DRESS,** 11:2-16

6. Concerning the **LORD'S TABLE,** 11:17-34

7. Concerning **SPIRITUAL GIFTS,** chs. 12-14

(1) **Endowment** of Gifts, ch. 12
   (a) Gifts are Given to Maintain Unity in Diversity, 12:1-11
   (b) Members of Human Body Compared to Gifts of Holy Spirit, 12:12-31
(2) **Energy** of Gifts—Love, ch. 13
(3) **Exercise** of Gifts, ch. 14
   (a) Gift of Prophecy is Superior to Gift of Tongues, 14:1-22
   (b) Order in Local Church for Exercise of Any Gift, 14:23-40

8. Concerning the **GOSPEL,** ch. 15

   (1) **Prominence** of Resurrection in the Gospel, 15:1-4
   (2) **Proofs** of Resurrection, 15:5-19
   (3) **Parade** of Resurrection, 15:20-28
      (a) Christ, the First Fruits
      (b) Those Who Are Christ's (Church)
      (c) Old Testament Saints, Tribulation Saints
      (d) Kingdom Set Up, Christ Reigning
      (e) Death Destroyed
      (f) Christ Returns to His Place in Trinity
   (4) **Program** and Pattern of Resurrection, 15:29-50
   (5) **Power** of Resurrection, 15:51-58

9. Concerning **COLLECTIONS,** 16:1-9

III. Closing Exhortations and Benediction, 16:10-24

II CORINTHIANS

Shortly after Paul had written 1 Corinthians from Ephesus, where he was in grave danger (2 Cor. 1:8), he wrote 2 Corinthians from Philippi. Paul was in Ephesus approximately 3 years. He had sent Titus to Corinth because he could not personally go there at that time. Timothy was with Paul in Ephesus and these two proceeded to Troas to wait for Titus to bring word from Corinth (2 Cor. 2:12, 13). When Titus did not come, Paul and Timothy went on to Philippi where Titus brought good news from Corinth (2 Cor. 7:5-11). Any breach between Paul and the Corinthian church was healed.

This Epistle is difficult to outline, as it is less organized than any of Paul's letters—but it contains more personal details. In each chapter there is always a minor theme developed which sometimes seems to take the place of the major theme, and is generally expressed in some striking verse. This may explain the seeming difficulty in outlining and organizing this Epistle. We will note this as we consider each chapter.

I Corinthians deals with conditions and *corrections* in the church.

II Corinthians deals with conditions of the *ministry* within the church.

OUTLINE:

I. COMFORT of God, chs. 1-7

(Christian Living)

1. Introduction, 1:1, 2
2. God's Comfort for Life's Plans, 1:3-24
3. God's Comfort in Restoring a Sinning Saint, ch. 2
4. God's Comfort in the Glorious Ministry of Christ, ch. 3
5. God's Comfort in the Ministry of Suffering for Christ, ch. 4
6. God's Comfort in the Ministry of Martyrdom for Christ, ch. 5
7. God's Comfort in All Circumstances of the Ministry of Christ, ch. 6
8. God's Comfort in the Heart of Paul, ch. 7

II. COLLECTION for the Poor Saints at Jerusalem, chs. 8, 9

(Christian Giving)

1. **Example** of Christian Giving, 8:1-6
2. **Exhortation** to Christian Giving, 8:7-15
3. **Explanation** of Christian Giving, 8:16-9:5
4. **Encouragement** to Christian Giving, 9:6-15

III. CALLING of the Apostle Paul, chs. 10-13

(Christian Guarding)

1. **Authentication** of Paul's Apostleship, ch. 10
2. **Vindication** of Paul's Apostleship, ch. 11
3. **Revelation** of Paul's Apostleship, ch. 12
4. **Execution** of Paul's Apostleship, 13:1-10
5. **Conclusion** of Paul's Apostleship, 13:11-14

RECOMMENDED BOOKS:

Grosheide, F. W.: *The First Epistle to the Corinthians.*
Hodge, Charles: *The Second Epistle to the Corinthians.*
Ironside, H. A.: *Addresses on the First Epistle to the Corinthians.*
Morgan, G. Campbell: *The Corinthian Letters of Paul.*
Pettingill, W. L.: *Simple Studies in I and II Corinthians.*
Robertson-Plummer: *International Critical Commentary.*
Sale-Harrison, L.: *The Judgment Seat of Christ.*

GALATIANS

WRITER: Paul

DATE: About A.D. 57

OCCASION:

Paul probably wrote this Epistle while on his third missionary journey during his two years at Ephesus. There is substantial basis, however, for the claim that it was written from Corinth, shortly before Paul wrote the Epistle to the Romans. Dr. Lenski advances the theory that it was written from Corinth on the second missionary journey, about April, A.D. 53.

Paul visited the Galatian churches on each of his three missionary journeys. There is no mention in the Epistle of another visit to the churches. The Epistle was evidently Paul's last word to these churches, written after he had visited them on the third missionary journey.

GALATIANS—the PEOPLE:

The destination of this Epistle has given rise to what is known as the North Galatian and the South Galatian theories. It seems more reasonable to suppose that it was sent to the churches in the area Paul visited on his first missionary journey, but this does not preclude the possibility that it had a wider circulation, even as far north as Pessinus, Ancyra, and Tavium. The word *Galatians* could be used in either an ethnographic sense, which would refer to the nationality of the people, or it could be used in a geographic sense which would refer to the Roman province by that name. Regardless of the position which is taken, there is a common blood strain which identified people in that area where there was a mixture of population. The people for whom the province was named were Gauls, a Celtic tribe from the same stock which inhabited France. In the 4th century B.C. they invaded the Roman Empire and sacked Rome. Later they crossed into Greece and captured Delphi in 280 B.C. At the invitation of Nikomedes I, King of Bithynia, they crossed over into Asia Minor to help him in a civil war. They were warlike people and soon established themselves in Asia Minor. In 189 B.C. they were made subjects of the Roman Empire and became a province. Their boundaries varied, and for many years they retained their customs and language. They were blond orientals. The churches Paul established on his first missionary journey were included at one time in the territory of Galatia, and this is the name which Paul would normally give to these churches.

These Gallic Celts had much of the same temperament and characteristics of the American population. Caesar had this to say, "The infirmity of the Gauls is, that they are fickle in their resolves, fond of show, but extremely inconstant, the fruit of excessive vanity." Remember that they wanted to make Paul a god one day, and the next day they stoned him (Acts 13, 14).

Surely the Epistle to the Galatians has a message for us, of like temper, who are beset on every hand by cults and isms innumerable that would take us, likewise, from our moorings in the Gospel of grace.

GALATIANS—the EPISTLE:

1. It is a stern, **severe,** and solemn message (Gal. 1:6-9; 3:1-5). It does not correct conduct, as the Corinthian letters do, but it is corrective—the Galatian believers were in grave peril. Because the foundations were being attacked, everything was threatened.

The Epistle contains no word of commendation, praise, or thanksgiving. There is no request for prayer, and there is no mention of their standing in Christ. No one with him is mentioned by name (1:2). Compare this with the other Epistles of Paul.

2. The heart of Paul the Apostle is laid bare, there is deep emotion and strong feeling. This is his **fighting Epistle**—he has on his war paint. He has no toleration for legalism. Someone has said that Romans comes from the head of Paul while Galatians comes from the heart of Paul. "Galatians takes up controversially what Romans puts systematically."

3. It is the **declaration of emancipation** from legalism of any type. This was Martin Luther's favorite Epistle, and it was on the masthead of the Reformation. It has been called the Magna Charta of the early church, the manifesto of Christian liberty, the im-

pregnable citadel, and a veritable Gibraltar against any attack on the heart of the Gospel. "Immortal victory is set upon its brow."

4. It is the strongest declaration and defense of the doctrine of **justification by faith** in or out of Scripture. It is God's polemic on behalf of the most vital truth of the Christian faith against any attack.

Not only is a sinner saved by grace through faith, but the saved sinner lives by grace. Grace is a way *to* life and a way *of* life.

OUTLINE:

I. INTRODUCTION, 1:1-10

1. Salutation—Cool Greeting, 1:1-5
2. Subject Stated—Warm Declamation, 1:6-10

II. PERSONAL —Authority of the Apostle and Glory of the Gospel, 1:11-2:14

1. Experience of Paul in Arabia, **1:11-24**
2. Experience of Paul with the Apostles in Jerusalem, **2:1-10**
3. Experience of Paul in Antioch with Peter, **2:11-14**

III. DOCTRINAL—Justification by Faith, 2:15-4:31

Faith vs. Works, Liberty vs. Bondage

1. Justification by Faith—Doctrine Stated, **2:15-21**
2. Justification by Faith—Experience of Galatians, **3:1-5**
3. Justification by Faith—Illustration of Abraham, **3:6-4:18**
4. Justification by Faith— Allegory of Hagar and Sarai, **4:19-31**

IV. PRACTICAL—Sanctification by the Spirit, 5:1-6:10

Spirit vs. Flesh, Liberty vs. Bondage

1. Saved by Faith and Living by Law
   Perpetrates Falling from Grace, **5:1-15**

2. Saved by Faith and Walking in the Spirit
   Produces Fruit of the Spirit, **5:16-26**
3. Saved by Faith and Fruit of the Spirit
   Presents Christian Character, **6:1-10**

V. AUTOGRAPHED CONCLUSION, 6:11-18

1. Paul's Own Handwriting, 6:11
2. Paul's Own Testimony, 6:12-18
   (1) Cross of Christ vs. Circumcision, 6:12-15
   (2) Christ's Handwriting on Paul's Body, 6:16-18
       (*The New Circumcision of the New Creation*)

RECOMMENDED BOOKS:

(See Matthew.)

Hogg and Vine: *The Epistle to the Galatians.*
Lenski, R. C.: *Interpretation of St. Paul's Epistles to the Galatians, Ephesians, and Philippians.*
Pettingill, W. L.: *Simple Studies in Galatians.*

A quartet of men left Rome in the year A.D. 62, bound for the province of Asia, which was located in what is currently designated as Asia Minor. These men had on their persons four of the most sublime compositions of the Christian faith. These precious documents would be invaluable if they were in existence today. Rome did not comprehend the significance of the writings of an unknown prisoner. If she had, these men would have been apprehended and the documents seized.

When they bade farewell to the Apostle Paul, each was given an epistle to bear to his particular constituency. These four letters are designated "the prison epistles of Paul" since he wrote them while imprisoned in Rome, awaiting a hearing before Nero, the Caesar at that time, to whom Paul, as a Roman citizen, had appealed his case.

This quartet of men and the respective places of abode can be identified:

(1) Epaphroditus from Philippi (Philippians 4:18) had the Epistle to the Philippians.

(2) Tychicus from Ephesus (Ephesians 6:21) had the Epistle to the Ephesians.

(3) Epaphras from Colosse (Colossians 4:12) had the Epistle to the Colossians.

(4) Onesimus, a slave from Colosse, (Philemon 10) had the Epistle to Philemon (who was his master).

These Epistles present a composite picture of Christ, the Church, the life, and the interrelationship and functioning of all. These different facets present the Chrisitian life on the highest plane.

EPHESIANS presents "the Church which is His body"—this is the invisible Church, of which Christ is the head.

COLOSSIANS presents Christ "the head of the body, the church." The emphasis is upon Christ, rather than on the Church.

PHILIPPIANS presents Christian living with Christ as the dynamic: "I can do all things through Christ which strengtheneth me" (Philippians 4:13).

PHILEMON presents Christian living in action in a pagan society: "If thou count me therefore a partner, receive him as myself. If he hath wronged thee, or oweth thee ought, put that on mine account" (Philemon 17, 18).

The Gospel walked in shoe leather in the first century—it worked.

In EPHESIANS Christ is exalted above all things "and hath put all things under his feet." Christ is the center of the circle of which the Church is the periphery.

In COLOSSIANS Christ is the fulness of God *(pleroma)*. He is the periphery of the circle of which Christian living is the center (Colossians 2:9, 10).

In PHILIPPIANS Christ is the center of the circle, the Christian living is the periphery. The *kenosis* is given (Philippians 2:5-8).

In PHILEMON Christ is both the center and circumference: "Hearing of thy love and faith, which thou hast toward the Lord Jesus, and toward all saints" (Philemon 5).

EPHESIANS   COLOSSIANS   PHILIPPIANS   PHILEMON

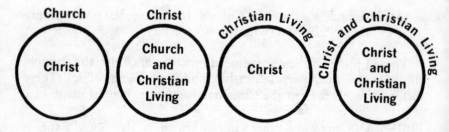

EPHESIANS

WRITER: Paul

DATE: Probably A.D. 62

Paul arrived in Rome in A.D. 61 as a prisoner, and for 2 years he lived in his own hired house where he received those who came to him (Acts 28: 16, 30).

THEME:

Ephesians reveals the Church as God's masterpiece (*poema*), see Ephesians 2:10, a mystery not revealed in the Old Testament. It is more wonderful than any temple made with hands, constructed of living stones, indwelt by the Holy Spirit (2:20-22). It is the body of Christ in the world—to walk as He would walk, and to wrestle against the wiles of the devil (1:22, 23; 4:1; 6:11, 12). Someday the Church will leave the world and be presented to Christ as a bride (5:25-32).

Dr. Pierson called Ephesians, "Paul's third-heaven epistle." Another has called it, "the Alps of the New Testament." It is the Mt. Whitney of the High Sierras of all Scripture. This is the *Church Epistle.*

TITLE:

The inscription *en Epheso* is omitted from the better manuscripts, and it is thought that the Epistle to the Ephesians was a circular epistle which included Ephesus and thereby explains the insertion of its name in some manuscripts. It is likewise thought that this Epistle is the one to the Laodiceans referred to in Colossians 4:16. This would correspond to the last of the seven letters to the churches in Revelation 2-3 rather than to the first church. The contents of the Ephesian letter correspond more to the condition of the Ephesian Church than to the one in Laodicea.

John Eadie concludes that this Epistle is Paul's Epistle to the church in Ephesus. He quotes from the testimony of the early

169

church to sustain this thesis (Irenaeus, Clement of Alexandria, Origen, Tertullian, Cyprian).

Ephesians is the great church Epistle, intended for all churches irrespective of geography; for the Church is "one body" and its location is "in the heavenlies."

PAUL AND EPHESUS:

The Holy Spirit forbade Paul, on his second missionary journey, to enter the province of Asia—where Ephesus was the prominent center (Acts 16:6).

He traveled west until he came to the sea, where it was necessary for God to direct him, by means of a vision, to Macedonia.

He was led by the Spirit into Europe as far as Corinth, after which he returned by way of Ephesus (Acts 18:19).

Being favorably impressed by the opportunities for missionary work, he promised to return. This he did on the 3rd missionary journey. He discovered that another, by the name of Apollos, had been there in the interval between his second and third missionary journeys; but he had preached only the baptism of John—not the Gospel of grace. Paul began a ministry there that was far-reaching. For two years he spoke in the school of Tyrannus, and the Gospel penetrated into every center of the province of Asia (Acts 19:8-10). Evidently it was at this time that the churches addressed in Revelation 2 and 3 were founded by this ministry of Paul.

This was probably the "high water mark" in the missionary labors of Paul. He considered Ephesus his great opportunity and stayed there longer than in any other place. The people of Ephesus heard more Bible teaching from Paul than did any other people, which is the reason he could write to them the deep truths contained in this Epistle (1 Corinthians 16:8, 9).

He met great opposition, but God marvelously preserved him, which encouraged him to continue (see Acts 19:23-41). Paul loved this church in Ephesus. His last meeting with the Ephesian elders was a tender farewell (see Acts 20:17-38).

Ephesus was the principal city of Asia Minor—and probably of the entire eastern section of the Roman Empire. It was virile and aggressive at this time, while the culture of Athens was decadent, and the commercialism of Corinth was corroded with immorality.

The temple of Diana was one of the seven wonders of the ancient world, being the largest Greek temple ever constructed (418 by 239 feet). It was built over a marsh on an artificial foundation of skins and charcoal so that it was not affected by earthquakes.

OUTLINE:

I. **DOCTRINAL**, the **Heavenly Calling** of the Church (Vocalization), **chs. 1-3**

A. The Church is a **BODY, ch. 1**

  1. Introduction, vv. 1, 2

  2. God the Father **Planned** the Church, vv. 3-6
  "a body hast thou prepared me"

  3. God the Son **Paid** the Price for the Church, vv. 7-12
  "redemption through his blood"

  4. God the Holy Spirit **Protects** the Church, vv. 13, 14
  "by one Spirit are we all baptized into one body"

  5. **Prayer** for Knowledge and Power, vv. 15-23

B. The Church is a **TEMPLE, ch. 2**

  1. The **Material** for Construction, vv. 1-10
  The "dead in trespasses" are made into a living temple

  2. The **Method** of Construction, vv. 11-18

  3. The **Meaning** of the Construction *(quo animo)*, vv. 19-22
  "groweth unto an holy temple in the Lord"

C. The Church is a **MYSTERY, ch. 3**

Ephesians

1. The **Explanation** of the Mystery, vv. 1-4
   Not revealed in the Old Testament

2. The **Definition** of the Mystery, vv. 5-13
   Jews and Gentiles are partakers of the same Body—the Church

3. **Prayer** for Power and Knowledge, vv. 14-21
   "strengthened with might" and *"to know the love of Christ"*

II. PRACTICAL, the **Earthly Conduct** of the Church (Vocation), **chs. 4-6**

A. The Church is a **NEW MAN, ch. 4**

1. The **Exhibition** of the New Man, vv. 1-6
   "endeavoring to keep the unity of the Spirit"

2. The **Inhibition** of the New Man, vv. 7-16
   "no more children" "grow up into Him" "perfect man"

3. The **Prohibition** of the New Man, vv. 17-32
   "walk not as other Gentiles walk" "be ye kind one to another"

B. The Church Will Be a **BRIDE, ch. 5**

1. The **Engagement** of the Church, vv. 1-17
   "for I have espoused you to one husband, that I may present you as a chaste virgin to Christ"

2. The **Experience** of the Church, vv. 18-24
   "be filled with the Spirit"

3. The **Expectation** of the Church, vv. 25-33
   "that he might present it to himself a glorious church"

C. The Church is a **SOLDIER, ch. 6**

1. The Soldier's **Relationships,** vv. 1-9

"no man that warreth entangleth himself with the affairs of this life"

2. The Soldier's **Enemy,** vv. 10-12
   "the wiles of the devil"

3. The Soldier's **Protection,** vv. 13-18
   "the whole armour of God"

4. The Soldier's **Example**—Paul, a Good Soldier of Jesus Christ, vv. 19-22

5. The Soldier's **Benediction,** vv. 23, 24

RECOMMENDED BOOKS:

(see Matthew list.)

Chafer, Lewis Sperry: *The Ephesian Letter.*
Eadie, John: *Commentary on the Epistle to the Ephesians.*
Gaebelein, A. C.: *His Riches.*
Harrison, Norman B.: *His Very Own.*
Ironside, H. A.: *In the Heavenlies.*
McGee, J. Vernon: *Exploring Through Ephesians.*

PHILIPPIANS

"The Earthly Walk of a Heavenly People"

WRITER: Paul

DATE: A.D. 62

Written at the same time as Ephesians, it is one of the Prison Epistles.

CITY OF PHILIPPI:

Philippi was a Roman colony. Although it was a miniature of Rome, and imitated and aped Rome in every way, it was none the less a city which had a higher cultural level than other cities visited by Paul.

CHURCH OF PHILIPPI:

1. It was less Jewish and more Gentile than were all others (the names of individuals mentioned are Greek and Roman). This was the first church established in Europe (Acts 16:6-40), which gives special meaning to Gentiles.

2. Women occupied a prominent place in this church. Paul attended, first of all, not the synagogue, but a prayer meeting of women (Acts 16:12-15). A woman named Lydia was the first convert in Europe. Two women were prominent in the church (Phil. 4:2), and there were others who labored in the church (Phil. 4:3).

3. It was generous in its gifts to the Lord's work (4:10-16). Paul cited them as examples to others in giving (2 Cor. 8:1-5).

OCCASION FOR EPISTLE:

There were two specific circumstances which occasioned the writing of this Epistle:

1. The church in Philippi kept in close touch with the apostle (Phil. 4:15), but apparently lost track of him when he was arrested in Jerusalem, and for two years there was no communication. They finally heard he was in prison in Rome, and immediately dispatched their pastor, Epaphroditus, to Rome with words of sympathy, a gift, and many expressions of love. Epaphroditus became ill in Rome, and, when he recovered, Paul wrote this letter and sent it by the messenger who brought him help.

2. A deeper reason was evidently the division which was arising because of the misunderstanding between two of the women (Phil. 4:2). One of the phrases which Paul used again and again is "you all," speaking to and of all of the believers in the church.

KEY:

The Epistle is practical; its key thought is *joy*. It has been labeled "the Secret of Joy." Some form of the word occurs 19 times. It answers the question, "How may I have joy in my heart?" The man who wrote, "Rejoice in the Lord always; and again I say, Rejoice," was in the Mamertine prison in Rome. Joy does not depend upon circumstances.

OUTLINE:

I. PHILOSOPHY for Christian Living, ch. 1

1. Introduction, vv. 1, 2
2. Paul's Tender Feeling for the Philippians, vv. 3-11
3. Bonds and Afflictions Further the Gospel, vv. 12-20
4. In Life or Death—Christ, vv. 21-30

II. PATTERN for Christian Living, ch. 2
(Key verses: 5-11)

1. Others, vv. 1-4
2. Mind of Christ—Humble, vv. 5-8
3. Mind of God—Exaltation of Christ, vv. 9-11
4. Mind of Paul—Things of Christ, vv. 12-18
5. Mind of Timothy—Likeminded with Paul, vv. 19-24
6. Mind of Epaphroditus—the Work of Christ, vv. 25-30

Philippians

III. PRIZE for Christian Living, ch. 3
(Key verses: 10-14)

1. Paul Changed His Bookkeeping System of the Past, vv. 1-9
2. Paul Changed His Purpose for the Present, vv. 10-19
3. Paul Changed His Hope for the Future, vv. 20, 21

IV. POWER for Christian Living, ch. 4
(Key verse: 13)

1. Joy—the Source of Power, vv. 1-4
2. Prayer—the Secret of Power, vv. 5-7
3. Contemplation of Christ—the Sanctuary of Power, vv. 8, 9
4. In Christ—the Satisfaction of Power, vv. 10-23

RECOMMENDED BOOKS:

(See Matthew list.)

Harrison, Norman B.: *His in Joyous Experience.*
Ironside, Harry A.: *Notes on Philippians.*
Sutcliffe, B. B.: *Rejoicing in the Lord.*

COLOSSIANS

WRITER: Paul

DATE: About A.D. 62 (one of the Prison Epistles)

CHURCH AT COLOSSE:

Paul had never been to Colosse when he wrote this Epistle (2:1). He was in Ephesus for about 2 years where he had his most fruitful ministry (see Acts 19:8-19). Colosse was 75 to 100 miles east of Ephesus, and visitors from Colosse had heard Paul and had come to know Christ. Apparently Philemon was one of these. A church came into existence in Colosse (Philemon 2). Paul intended to visit there when he was released from prison (Philemon 22). Paul wrote to this church as though it were his own.

Epaphras was the minister of the Colossian church (1:4-8; 4:12, 13).

PROBLEM AT COLOSSE:

Colosse, located in southwest Phrygia in Asia Minor, near Laodicea, was beset with oriental mysticism. Gnosticism had evidently intruded with its Greek pantheistic philosophy of the demiurge.

GNOSTICISM	PAUL'S ANSWER
(1) They had an exclusive spirit (were aristocratic in wisdom).	1:28
(2) They held speculative tenets on creation—that God did not create the universe directly, but created a creature who in turn created another creature, until one finally created the physical universe. Christ was considered a creature in this long series of creations.	1:15-19; 2:18

177

GNOSTICISM	PAUL'S ANSWER
(3) Their ethical practice was asceticism (influenced by Greek Stoicism), and unrestrained licentiousness (from Greek Epicureanism).	2:16, 23 3:5-9

MESSAGE OF COLOSSIANS:

Colossians is the chart and compass which enables the believer to sail between the ever present Scylla and Charybdis. "Pure Christianity lives between two dangers ever present: the danger that it will evaporate into a philosophy—philosophies of the atonement... and the danger that it will freeze into a form" (Dr. Scofield). Jesus said that He is the water of life. He did not say that He was the ice of life; He did not say that He was the steam of life. We are not to add something to Christ nor subtract from Him.

The message of this Epistle can best be seen by comparing it with other Prison Epistles.

Subject: Ephesians—the body of believers, called the Church, of which Christ is the Head.

Colossians—the Head of the body who is Christ; the body is only secondary (1:18).

Theme: Philippians—Christian living is the theme and periphery of the circle (see p. 168) where Christ is the center.

Colossians—Christ is the theme and the periphery of the circle where Christian living is the center.

Philippians emphasizes the *kenosis*—Christ became a Servant (Phil. 2:7).

Colossians emphasizes the *pleroma*—Christ is the fulness of God (Col. 2:9).

"Thou, O Christ, art all I want; more than all in Thee I find" (Charles Wesley).

OUTLINE:

I. Doctrinal, chs. 1, 2
Christ, the fulness (pleroma) of God; in Christ we are made full.

1. Introduction, 1:1-8
2. Paul's Prayer, 1:9-14
3. Person of Christ, 1:15-19
4. Objective Work of Christ for Sinners, 1:20-23
5. Subjective Work of Christ for Saints, 1:24-29
6. Christ, the Answer to Philosophy, 2:1-15
   (For the HEAD)
7. Christ, the Answer to Ritual, 2:16-23
   (For the HEART)

II. Practical, chs. 3, 4
Christ, the fulness of God, poured out in life through believers. (Breaking the alabaster box of ointment in the world.)

1. Thoughts and Affections of Believers are Heavenly, 3:1-4
   (The believer's heart should be in heaven where his Head is.)
2. Living of Believers is Holy, 3:5-4:6
   (In all relationships, personal, social, marital, parental, capital and labor, the believer should manifest Christ.)
3. Fellowship of Believers is Hearty, 4:7-18
   (Roster of faithful workers similar to Rom. 16 & Heb. 11)

RECOMMENDED BOOKS:

(See Matthew list.)

English, E. Schuyler: *Studies in the Epistle to the Colossians.*
Ironside, H. A.: *Lectures on Colossians.*
Moule, H. C. G.: *Colossians and Philemon Studies.*
Thomas, W. H. Griffith: *Christ Pre-eminent.*

I THESSALONIANS

WRITER: Paul

DATE: A.D. 52-53

PLACE:

Thessalonica was a Roman colony and very important in the life of the Roman Empire. It was located 100 miles west of Philippi and north of Athens about half that distance. It was the chief city of Macedonia. Cicero said, "Thessalonica is in the bosom of the Empire."

It was first named Therma because of hot springs in that area. In 316 B.C. Cassander (who succeeded Alexander the Great) named it in memory of his wife, Thessalonike, a half sister of Alexander the Great. Thessalonica is still in existence and the present day name is Salonika.

The church in Thessalonica was a model church. Paul cited it to the Corinthians as an example (see 1:7; 2 Cor. 8:1-5).

OCCASION:

This was the earliest Epistle written by Paul. It was written from Athens or, more likely, Corinth on his second missionary journey. Paul had to leave Thessalonica "post-haste" due to the great opposition to the Gospel. The enemy pursued him to Berea, and again Paul was forced to leave. He left Silas and Timothy at Berea, but he went on to Athens. It was evidently there that Timothy brought him word from the church in Thessalonica (3:6), together with some questions that they had raised. Paul wrote this first Epistle in response to their overture.

THEME:

Although Paul was in Thessalonica less than a month (Acts 17:2), he touched on many of the great doctrines of the church.

Among them was the second coming of Christ. This theme was not above the heads of the new converts, according to the great apostle. The particular phase in the second coming of Christ which he emphasized was Christ's coming for believers. The second coming of Christ in relationship to believers is a comfort (I Thes. 4:18). This aspect is quite different from His catastrophic and cataclysmic coming in glory to establish His kingdom by putting down all unrighteousness (Rev. 19:11-16).

PURPOSE:

1. To *confirm* young converts in the elementary truth of the Gospel.
2. To *condition* them to go on unto holy living,
3. To *comfort* them regarding the return of Christ.

A heathen inscription in Thessalonica reads:

"After death no reviving,
After the grave no meeting again."

OUTLINE:

I. The Christian's **Attitude** toward the Return of Christ, **ch. 1** (to serve...to wait...vv. 9, 10)

II. The Christian's **Reward** at the Return of Christ, **ch. 2**

III. The Christian's **Life** and the Return of Christ, **3:1-4:**12

IV. The Christian's **Death** and the Return of Christ, **4:**13-18

V. The Christian's **Actions** in View of Return of Christ, **ch. 5** (Note 22 specific commands to Christians, beginning at v. 11.)

For this book we are suggesting two outlines. Each one gives a needed emphasis that is not in the other.

I. **Coming of Christ is an INSPIRING HOPE, ch. 1**

1. Introduction, vv. 1-4

2. Gospel Received in Much Assurance & Much Affliction, vv. 5-7
3. Gospel Results: Turned from Idols to God; Wait for Coming of Christ, vv. 8-10

II. Coming of Christ is a WORKING HOPE, ch. 2

1. Motive & Method of a True Witness for Christ, vv. 1-6
2. Mother-Side of the Apostle's Ministry (Comfort), vv. 7-9
3. Father-Side of the Apostle's Ministry (Charge), vv. 10-13
4. Brother-Side of the Apostle's Ministry (Challenge), vv. 14-16
5. Reward of a True Witness for Christ, vv. 17-20

III. Coming of Christ is a PURIFYING HOPE, 3:1-4:12
Sanctification

1. Timothy Brings Good Report of Thessalonians, vv. 1-8
2. Paul Urges Thessalonians to
   Continue to Grow in Faith, vv. 9-13
3. How Believers Are to Walk, 4:1-12

IV. Coming of Christ is a COMFORTING HOPE, 4:13-18
*(What Death Means to a Christian
What the Rapture Means to the Church)*

V. Coming of Christ is a ROUSING HOPE, ch. 5
Leads to Action

*Dead Believers Are Asleep in Jesus
Living Believers Are Awake for Jesus*

1. Call to be Awake & Alert in View of Christ's Coming, vv. 1-10
2. Commandments for Christians, vv. 11-28

This section is practical. We need to watch our step as we look up for the coming of Christ.

RECOMMENDED BOOKS:

Hogg & Vine: *The Epistles to the Thessalonians.*
Ironside, H. A.: *Addresses in the I & II Thessalonians.*
Pettingill, W. L.: *Simple Studies in I & II Thessalonians.*
Walvoord, John F.: *The Thessalonian Epistles.*

II THESSALONIANS

WRITER: Paul

DATE: A.D. 52-53 (The 2nd Epistle followed shortly after the 1st).

OCCASION:

The first letter to the Thessalonians had given rise to further questions, and Paul is attempting to answer these. There was circulating in the Thessalonian church a letter or report, purported to have come from Paul, which was inclined to disturb the Christians. This false report claimed that Christ had already come and had already gathered out the Church to Himself, and that the world was then living in the judgments of the "day of the Lord." Their present persecutions confirmed this false report. Paul attempts to allay their fears by stating definitely that "our gathering together unto Him" is yet future (2:1), and that "the day of the Lord" has certain forerunners which must first come. The apostasy and the "man of sin" must come first; the removal of the remnant of believers at "our gathering together unto Him" makes the apostasy in the professing church 100% (Luke 18:8).

Every era of persecution or trouble has given rise to the false impression that the Church is going through the time of judgment which Christ identified as the "great tribulation" (Matt. 24:21). This period has been so clearly identified by Christ that there is no reason for getting panicky and for being stampeded into an unwarranted position. Christ said that there is coming a small interval which will be blocked off by "such as was not since the beginning of the world to this time, no, nor ever shall be." Nothing like it has taken place before, and nothing like it will ever take place afterward. Has there ever been such a period of unparalleled trouble? The answer is obvious.

THEME:

The first Epistle to the Thessalonians relates the return of Christ to that phase where He returns to the earth in judgment, and where one of the accomplishments is in connection with the "man of sin," whom He "shall destroy with the brightness of His coming." These two aspects are clearly delineated. The interval between these two phases is the Great Tribulation, which can be further identified with the 70th week of Daniel 9 as a period of seven years.

THE DAY OF THE LORD:

This is the phrase which occurs in 2:2 (incorrectly translated "the day of Christ" in the Authorized Version). It is an Old Testament phrase with definite connotations. It occurs in the writings of the Old Testament prophets where it relates to the future kingdom promised in the Old Testament. *The day of Christ* is a New Testament expression (1 Cor. 1:8); it relates here to the future of the Church. *The day of the Lord* is connected with the coming of Christ as it relates to the setting up of the kingdom. The day of Christ is cónnected with the coming of Christ for the Church. Whatever else is implied in these two statements, certainly this is basic.

The teaching in 1 Thessalonians is that the saints who have died will have part in Christ's coming for His living saints; in 2 Thessalonians it is that the saints who are alive will not have part in the Great Tribulation. The return of Christ has a peculiar and precious meaning for His saints.

OUTLINE:

I. **PERSECUTION of Believers Now;**
   Judgment of Unbelievers Hereafter
   (at Coming of Christ), 1:1-12

   1. Introduction, 1:1,2
   2. **Persecution** of Believers and Fruits of It, 1:3-7
   3. **Judgment** of Wicked at Coming of Christ, 1:8-12

II. **PROGRAM for World**
   in Connection with Coming of Christ, 2:1-12

   1. **Rapture** Occurs First, 2:1

2. **Day of Lord** Follows; Introduced by Total Apostasy & Appearance of Man of Sin, 2:2-5

3. **Mystery of Lawlessness** Working Today; Lawless One Restrained by Holy Spirit, 2:6-8

4. **Lawless One** to Appear in Great Tribulation Period, 2:9-12

III. PRACTICALITY of Coming of Christ, 2:13-3:18

1. Believers Should Be Established in **Word**, 2:13-17
2. Believers Should Be Established in **Walk**, 3:1-7
3. Believers Should Be Established in **Work**, 3:8-18

RECOMMENDED BOOKS:

Hogg & Vine: *The Epistles to the Thessalonians.*
Ironside, H. A.: *Addresses in the I & II Thessalonians.*
Pettingill, W. L.: *Simple Studies in I & II Thessalonians.*
Walvoord, John F.: *The Thessalonian Epistles.*

The two letters to Timothy and the one to Titus are labeled Pastoral Epistles. The contents of the letters reveal the obvious reason for this. They were written by Paul to two of his young converts (1 Tim. 1:2; Titus 1:4), who had followed him on many of his missionary journeys, and whom he had established as pastors of churches at the time of the writing of these Epistles. He gave instructions for the orderly procedure of local and visible churches. These letters have a particular message to young pastors, and they have pertinent instructions for the present day church. Although they were addressed by Paul to his young friends in the ministry, not to churches, the message is for churches.

I TIMOTHY

WRITER: Paul

DATE: About A.D. 64

Probably Paul was released from prison at Rome between A.D. 64 and 67. If this is accurate, it was during this interval that he wrote this first Epistle to Timothy. Also he wrote to Titus at this same time. Some authorities think that Paul wrote from Macedonia. Apparently he had left Timothy in Ephesus (1 Tim. 1:3), and he wrote this letter to encourage and to assist him (1 Tim. 6:20).

THEME: Government and order in the local church.

This is in contrast to the Epistle to the Ephesians where the Church is the Body of Christ, the invisible Church. Here it is a local assembly of believers organized for a common purpose.

KEY VERSES: 1 Tim. 1:3; 3:15

Sound doctrine and correct conduct identify the local church.

Doctrine occurs 8 times;
Godliness occurs 8 times;
Teach and *teacher* occur 7 times;
Good occurs 22 times.

OUTLINE:

I. THE FAITH of the Church, ch. 1

1. Introduction, vv. 1, 2
2. Warning against Unsound Doctrine, vv. 3-10
3. Personal Testimony of Paul vv. 11-17
4. Charge to Timothy, vv. 18-20

II. PUBLIC PRAYER and WOMAN'S PLACE in the Churches, ch. 2

1. Public Prayer for the Public and Public Officials, vv. 1-7
2. How Men are to Pray, v. 8
3. How Women are to Pray, vv. 9-15

III. OFFICERS in the Churches, ch. 3

1. Requirements for Elders, vv. 1-7
2. Requirements of Deacons, vv. 8-13
3. Report of Paul to Timothy, vv. 14-16

IV. APOSTASY in the Churches, ch. 4

1. How to Recognize the Apostates, vv. 1-5
2. What the "Good Minister" Can Do in Times of Apostasy, vv. 6-16

V. DUTIES of OFFICERS of the Churches, chs. 5, 6

1. Relationship of Ministers
   to Different Groups in the Local Church, ch. 5
2. Relationships of Believers to Others, ch. 6

RECOMMENDED BOOKS:

Vincent, Marvin R.: *Word Studies in the New Testament,* Vol. IV.

II TIMOTHY

WRITER: Paul

DATE: A.D. 67

The following is a probable calendar of the events of Paul's life during his last years:

A.D. 58   Paul's arrest in Jerusalem.
A.D. 61   His arrival in Rome.
A.D. 61-63   His first Roman imprisonment.
A.D. 64-67   His release. He writes 1 Timothy and Titus from
             Macedonia.
A.D. 67-68   His arrest and death. He writes 2 Timothy prior to
             his death in Rome.

KEY VERSES: 2 Tim. 2:15; 4:2

Key words are *ashamed* (1:8, 12), and *endure* (2:3).

THEME: Loyalty in days of apostasy.

1. Loyalty in suffering (ch. 1)
2. Loyalty in service (ch. 2)
3. Loyalty in apostasy (chs. 3-4:5)
4. Lord loyal to His servants in desertion (4:6-4:22)

REMARKS:

Webster's definition of apostasy is: *total desertion of principles of faith.* Apostasy is not due to ignorance; it is a heresy. Apostasy is deliberate error, it is intentional departure from the faith. An apostate is one who knows the truth of the Gospel (doctrines of the faith).

In 2 Timothy Paul speaks of the ultimate outcome of Gospel preaching. The final fruition will not be the total conversion of mankind, nor will it usher in the Millennium. On the contrary, there will come about an apostasy which will well-nigh blot out "the faith" from the earth. This is in complete harmony with the startling word of Christ, "When the Son of man cometh, shall he find faith on the earth?" This is not in keeping, of course, with a social gospel which expects to transform the world by tinkering with the social system. These vain optimists have no patience with the doleful words of 2 Timothy. Nevertheless, the cold and hard facts of history and the events of the present hour demonstrate the accuracy of Paul. We are now in the midst of an apostasy which is cut to the pattern of Paul's words in remarkable detail.

Although the visible church has entered the orbit of awful apostasy, the invisible Church is on its way to the epiphany of glory.

SPECIAL FEATURE: "Swan Song" of the Apostle

The deathbed statement of any individual has an importance which is not attached to other remarks. This is what lends significance to 2 Timothy. It is the deathbed communication of Paul; it is his final message. It has a note of sadness which is not detected in his other Epistles. Nevertheless, there is the overtone of triumph, "I have fought a good fight, I have finished my course...." Paul writes his own epitaph in 4:6-8. The Epistle is very personal—there are 25 references to individuals.

OUTLINE:

I. AFFLICTIONS of the Gospel, ch. 1

1. Introduction, 1:1-7
2. Not Ashamed, but a Partaker of Affliction, 1:8-11
3. Not Ashamed, but Assured, 1:12-18

II. ACTIVE in Service, ch. 2

1. A Good Soldier, 2:1-14
2. A Good Student, 2:15-26

III. APOSTASY Coming; Authority of the Scriptures, 3:1-4:5

1. Conditions in the Last Days, 3:1-9
2. Authority of Scriptures in the Last Days, 3:10-17

II Timothy

    3. Instructions for the Last Days, 4:1-5

IV. ALLEGIANCE to the Lord and of the Lord, 4:6-22

    1. Deathbed Testimony of Paul, 4:6-8
    2. Last Words, 4:9-22
       ("The Lord stood with me.")

RECOMMENDED BOOKS:

Ironside, H. A.: *Timothy, Titus, and Philemon.*
Vincent, Marvin R.: *Word Studies in the New Testament.*

TITUS

WRITER: Paul

DATE: A.D. 64-67 (see notes on 1 Timothy).

CONTRAST:

While little is known of either Timothy or Titus, there seems
to have been quite a contrast between them. Titus seems to have
been a stronger man, both physically and spiritually, since Paul expresses less concern for his welfare. Titus was probably more mature, and possessed a virile personality. Timothy was a Jew who
was circumcised by Paul, but Titus was a Gentile, and Paul seems
to have refused to circumcise him (Gal. 2:3). Paul circumcised one
young preacher and refused to circumcise the other. Surely there
is no rule that can be drawn from this, other than "in Christ Jesus
neither circumcision availeth anything, nor uncircumcision; but a
new creation" (Gal. 6:15).

THE NEW TESTAMENT CHURCH:

Here is a fine picture of the New Testament church in its full-
orbed realization in the community as an organization. Many boast
today that they belong to a New Testament church. In this Epistle
is found the measuring rod. The ideal church is one that has an
orderly organization, is sound in doctrine, pure in life, and "ready
to every good work."

THE RETURN OF CHRIST:

In the first two Epistles which Paul wrote, the return of Christ
is a great pulsating hope (1, 2 Thessalonians). This has led some
critics to say that Paul believed this only when he was young, and
that he changed when he became more mature. However, in this
Epistle to Titus, one of his last, the blessed hope still possesses
the soul of this intrepid pioneer of faith, "Looking for that blessed
hope, and the glorious appearing of the great God and our Savior
Jesus Christ" (Tit. 2:13). The word for *looking* has the root mean-

ing of *entertaining*. This is the hope which occupied the guest chamber in the heart of Paul during all of his life, beginning at the Damascus Road and going on to the Appian Way.

OUTLINE:

I. **The Church is an Organization, ch. 1**
   (As such, it should be orderly [v. 5].)

   1. Introduction, vv. 1-4
   2. An Orderly Church Must Have Ordained Elders Who Meet Prescribed Requirements, vv. 5-9
   3. The Bad Reputation of the Cretans, vv. 10-16

II. **The Church is to Teach and Preach the Word of God, ch. 2**

   1. The Church Must Teach Sound Doctrine, vv. 1-10
   2. The Church Must Preach the Grace of God, vv. 11-15

III. **The Church is to Perform Good Works, ch. 3**
   (To do this, it should be eager, anxious, and learning to perform good works [vv. 1, 8, 14].)

   1. Good Works are Evidence of Salvation, vv. 1-7
      (The works of the Holy Spirit.)
   2. Good Works are Profitable for the Present and Future, vv. 8-15

RECOMMENDED BOOKS:

(See Matthew.)

Ironside, H. A.: *Timothy, Titus, and Philemon.*

PHILEMON

WRITER: Paul

DATE: Probably A.D. 62 (see outline of Ephesians, the Prison Epistles introduction).

FORM:

The Epistles present a different style in revelation. God had used law, history, poetry, prophecy, and the Gospels heretofore, but in the Epistles, He adopted a more personal and direct method. In this intimate way, He looks back to the cross and talks about the church. Someone has said that the Epistles are the love letters of Christ to us. The Epistle of Philemon is individual and intimate. There is reason to believe that Paul did not expect its contents to be divulged (at other times he knew that he was writing Scripture). This does not detract from the inspiration and value of Philemon, but rather enhances its value and message.

BACKGROUND:

The story behind the Epistle to Philemon was enacted on the black background of slavery. There were approximately 60 million slaves in the Roman Empire where the total population did not exceed 120 million. A slave was a chattel. He was treated worse than an enemy, and was subject to the whim of his master.

The story can be briefly reconstructed. Onesimus was a slave belonging to Philemon, a Christian of Colosse. This slave had opportunity to run away, and seized upon it. He made his way to Rome where he expected his identity and past life to be swallowed up by the great metropolis. One day he chanced upon a gathering where Paul was preaching. There he heard the Gospel of the Lord Jesus Christ, and the Holy Spirit regenerated him, making him a new creature in Christ. He told his story to Paul, and Paul sent him back to Philemon with this accompanying letter.

Philemon

PURPOSE:

The **primary** purpose of this Epistle is to reveal Christ's love for us in what He did for us before God in pleading our case. This is the finest illustration of substitution. "If he hath wronged thee, or oweth thee ought, put that on mine account" (v. 18). We can hear Christ agreeing to take our place and to have all our sin imputed to Him—"For he hath made him to be sin for us..." (2 Cor. 5:21a). He took our place in death, but He gives us His place in life: "If thou count me therefore a partner, receive him as myself" (v. 17). We have the standing of Christ before God, or we have none at all. He took our hell, and He gives us His heaven—...that we might be made the righteousness of God in him" (2 Cor. 5:21b). Onesimus, an unprofitable run-away slave, was to be received as Paul, the great apostle, would have been received in the home of Philemon.

The **practical** purpose is to teach brotherly love. Paul spoke of the new relationship between master and servant in the other Prison Epistles. Here he demonstrates how it should work. These men, belonging to two different classes in the Roman Empire, hating each other and hurting each other, are now brothers in Christ—and they are to act like it. This is the only solution to the problem of capital and labor.

OUTLINE:

1. **Genial greeting** to Philemon and His Family, vv. 1-3
2. **Good Reputation** of Philemon, vv. 4-7
3. **Gracious Plea** for Onesimus, vv. 8-16
4. **Guiltless Substitutes** for Guilty, v. 17
5. **Glorious Illustration** of Imputation, v. 18
6. **General and Personal** Items and Requests, vv. 19-25

RECOMMENDED BOOKS:

Gaebelein, Frank E.: *Philemon.*
Ironside, H. A.: *Timothy, Titus, and Philemon.*
Moule, H. C. G.: *Colossians & Philemon Studies.*

HEBREWS

WRITER: Paul (?)

Although the Authorized Version has the heading "Epistle of Paul the Apostle to the Hebrews," there is still a question as to authorship. The American Revised Version corrects this and gives the heading "The Epistle to the Hebrews." In spite of the fact that the Pauline authorship cannot be made in a dogmatic fashion, there is abundant evidence that Paul was the author. Both internal and external evidence support the authorship of Paul. The writer had been in bonds (10:34). He wrote from Italy (13:24); his companion was Timothy (13:23). The writing is Pauline. In my opinion Peter identifies Paul as the writer (2 Pet. 3:15, 16; 1 Pet. 1:1).

DATE: Before A.D. 70

Heb. 10:11 reveals that it was written before the destruction of the Temple by Titus in A.D. 70.

THEME:

Coleridge said that Romans revealed the *necessity* of the Christian faith, but that Hebrews revealed the *superiority* of the Christian faith. This thought is expressed in the use of the comparative word *better,* which occurs 13 times. Here are some other words which express the theme:

Perfect —occurs 15 times (cognate words);
Let us —occurs 13 times;
Let —occurs 5 times.

Two verses, likewise, convey this "better" way: Heb. 3:1; 12:3.

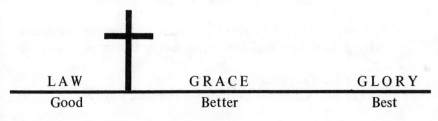

LAW	GRACE	GLORY
Good	Better	Best

Hebrews

SUBJECT: The superiority of Christ

OUTLINE:

(3) New Sanctuary Better than the Old, 9:1-10
(4) Superior Sacrifice, 9:11-10:18
(5) Encouragement, 10:19-25

5th Danger Signal: Peril of Despising, 10:26-39

II. CHRIST BRINGS BETTER BENEFITS & DUTIES, chs. 11-13
(Practical)

1. **Faith,** 11:1-40
2. **Hope,** 12:1-29

(1) The Christian Race, 12:1, 2
(2) Believers are Now in Contest & Conflict, 12:3-14

6th Danger Signal: Peril of Denying, 12:15-29

3. **Love,** 13:1-25

(1) Secret Life of Believers, 13:1-6
(2) Social Life of Believers, 13:7-14
(3) Spiritual Life of Believers, 13:15-19

RECOMMENDED BOOKS:

(See Matthew.)

Meyer, F. B.: *The Way Into The Holiest.*
Morgan, G. Campbell: *God's Last Word to Man.*
Pettingill, W. L.: *Into the Holiest.*
Ridout, S.: *Lectures on Hebrews.*
Saphir, A.: *The Epistle to the Hebrews.*
Thomas, W. H. Griffith: *Let Us Go On.*

James, 1 & 2 Peter, 1, 2, & 3 John, and Jude are designated as "catholic" epistles in the sense of "universal" because they are not addressed to a particular individual or church, but to the Church as a whole.

JAMES

WRITER: James

The problem of authorship is a major one. Some find at least 4 men by the name of James in the New Testament. At least 3 are clearly identified:

1. James, brother of John, son of Zebedee, called by our Lord "son of thunder." He was slain by Herod (Acts 12:1, 2).

2. James, son of Alphaeus, called "James the less." He is mentioned in the list of apostles, but very little is known concerning him.

3. James, the Lord's brother (Matt. 13:55; Mk. 6:3), in reality a half brother according to the flesh. He became head of the church at Jerusalem (Acts 15:13). This James is evidently the writer of this Epistle (Gal. 2:9).

DATE: A.D. 45-50

This was the first book of the New Testament to be written. Some have taken the position that James wrote to combat the writings of Paul. It is obvious that this is an erroneous position since none of Paul's epistles were in existence at the time of this writing.

JAMES AND PAUL:

The seeming contradiction between James and Paul can be easily explained when the message of James is considered. James takes the position, as does Paul, that we are justified by faith, but that the faith which justifies produces good works. Calvin said, "Faith alone saves, but the faith that saves is not alone." Justification is shown by works—not justified *by,* but *for* good works. James and Paul present the two aspects of justification by faith.

Paul emphasized both phases:

Faith—not justified *by* works (Eph. 2:8, 9; Tit. 3:5)

Works—justified *for* works (Tit. 3:8; Eph. 2:10)

Faith is the root of salvation—works are the fruit of salvation.
Faith is the cause of salvation—works are the result of salvation.

KEY VERSES: Jas. 1:22 and 2:20

THEME: Ethics of Christianity, not doctrine.

The Epistle of James has been compared to the book of Proverbs in the Old Testament. Both emphasize the practical. In both there is the learning experience for the child of God.

Justification by faith is demonstrated by works. Justification by faith is poured into the test tube of:
    Works—Chapters 1, 2
    Words—Chapter 3
    Worldliness—Chapter 4
    Warning to the Rich—Chapter 5

OUTLINE:

  I. **VERIFICATION of Genuine Faith, chs. 1-3**

      1. God Tests Faith by Trials, 1:1-12
         (Twofold result: development of patience here, v. 3; reward hereafter, v. 12.)

      2. God Does Not Test Faith with Evil, 1:13-21
         (Evil comes from within—the flesh, v. 14.)

3. God Tests Faith by THE WORD, Not by Man's Words, 1:22-27
   (Doing, not doctrine, is the final test of faith; knowing is not enough.)

4. God Tests Faith by Attitude & Action in Respect of Persons, 2:1-13

5. God Tests Faith by Good Works, 2:14-26
   (Abraham is an illustration of works, v. 21.)

6. God Tests Faith by the Tongue, ch. 3
   ("What is in the well of the heart will come up through the bucket of the mouth.")

II. **VACUITY and VAPIDNESS of Worldliness, ch. 4**
   (Worldliness is identified with fighting and the spirit of dissension, vv. 1, 2.)

III. **VEXATION of the Rich;**
   VALUE of the Imminent Coming of Christ, ch. 5

   (The soon coming of Christ produces patience, vv. 7, 8 and prayer, vv. 13-18.)

   1. Riches Are a Care (Rich Warned), 5:1-6

   2. Coming of Christ is a Comfort, 5:7-12

   3. Prayer of the Righteous is a Power, 5:13-20

RECOMMENDED BOOKS:

(See Matthew.)

Grant, F. W.: *The Numerical Bible.*
Ironside, Harry A.: *Notes on James and Peter.*
Strauss, Lehman: *James Your Brother.*
Vincent, Marvin R.: *Word Studies in the New Testament,* Vol. I
Zodhiates, S.: *The Work of Faith.*

I PETER

WRITER: Simon Peter

Peter has been called the ignorant fisherman, but no man who had spent three years in the school of Jesus could be called ignorant, and the Epistles of Peter confirm this.

A great change is seen in the life of Peter from these Epistles. He had been impetuous, but now he is patient. The transforming power of the Gospel had wrought this change in his life.

DATE: A.D. 64-67

Peter wrote his two Epistles and was put to death sometime during this period. 1 Peter was written, evidently, around A.D. 64, and 2 Peter a short time later.

PLACE: Babylon

Although the place from which it was written has been the pre-eminent problem of this Epistle, it is given as Babylon (5:13). Many treat this in a metaphorical sense as meaning Rome. However the legend that Peter was in Rome for 25 years preceding his martyrdom is grounded in the apocryphal writings of the heretical Ebionites.

The list of countries in 1 Peter 1:1 is from east to west, which suggests that the writer was in the east at the time of writing. Furthermore, Babylon is directly mentioned as the origin, and this Epistle was written before Rome was called Babylon in a symbolic way. If Peter had meant Rome, the chances are that he would have said *Rome.* There was at this time a large colony of Jews in ancient Babylon who had fled Rome due to severe persecution under Claudius, and at the time of writing bloody Nero was on the throne. This is in harmony with the theme of the Epistle. In spite of the fact that Papias mentions the death of Peter as occurring in Rome, there is no substantial historical basis for this supposition.

I Peter

THEME: Christian hope in the time of trial

Peter deals with doctrine and handles weighty subjects. This is seen in his treatment of the great words of the Gospel, many of which are gathered together at the outset (v. 2): *elect, foreknowledge, sanctification, obedience, blood,* and the *Trinity.* He used some of these words several times. Added to these are: *salvation* (used 3 times), *revelation* (with cognate words, used 5 times), *glory* (with cognate words, used 16 times), *faith* (5 times), and *hope* (4 times).

Peter has been called the apostle of hope; Paul, the apostle of faith; John, the apostle of love.

The word that conveys the theme, however, is *suffering* (which, with cognate words, occurs 16 times). The word *hope* is tied to it— the Christian hope in the time of trial.

OUTLINE:

I. **SUFFERING and the SECURITY of Believers, 1:1-9**
   Produces Joy

II. **SUFFERING and the SCRIPTURES, 1:10-25**
   Produces Holiness

III. **SUFFERING and the SUFFERING of CHRIST, chs. 2-4**
   1. Produces Separation, ch. 2
   2. Produces Christian Conduct, ch. 3
      (1) Conduct in the Home, 3:1-7
      (2) Conduct in the Church, 3:8-17
      (3) Christ's Suffering Preached
          by the Spirit in Noah's Day, 3:18-22
   3. Produces Obedience to the Will of God, ch. 4

IV. **SUFFERING and the SECOND COMING of Christ, ch. 5**
   1. Produces Service and Hope, 5:1-4
   2. Produces Humility and Patience, 5:5-14

RECOMMENDED BOOKS:

Brown, John: *Expository Discourses on 1 Peter.*
Cramer, George H.: *First and Second Peter.*
Ironside, H. A.: *James and Peter.*
Meyer, F. B.: *Tried by Fire.*
Niebor, J.: *First and Second Epistle of Peter.*
Stibbs, Alan M.: *The First Epistle General of Peter. Tyndale New Testament Commentaries.*
Wuest, Kenneth S.: *First Peter in the Greek New Testament.*

II PETER

WRITER: Simon Peter

The Petrine authorship has been challenged more than the authorship of any other book in the New Testament. Dr. Moorehead said, "The Second Epistle of Peter comes to us with less historical support of its genuineness than any other book of the New Testament." However, this has caused conservative scholars to give adequate attention to this Epistle so that today it is well established that Peter wrote this letter. The autobiographical sections afford internal evidence of the Petrine authorship (see 2 Pet. 1:13, 14; 1:16-18; 3:1).

DATE: About A.D. 66

This second Epistle was written shortly after his first Epistle (3:1), and a short while before his martyrdom (1:13, 14).

THEME:

This is the "swan song" of Peter, as 2 Timothy is the "swan song" of Paul. There is a striking similarity. Both Epistles put up a warning sign, along the pilgrim pathway the church is traveling, to identify the awful apostasy that was on the way at that time, and now in our time has arrived. What was then like a cloud the size of a man's hand, today envelops the sky and produces a storm of hurricane proportions. Peter warns of heresy among teachers, as Paul warns of heresy among the laity. Both Peter and Paul speak in a joyful manner of their approaching death (2 Pet. 1:13, 14; 2 Tim. 4:6-8). Both apostles anchor the church on the Scriptures as the only defense against the coming storm.

The similarity of 2 Peter to Paul's last epistle of 2 Timothy explains the sharp contrast between Peter's first and second letters. The subject has changed and the difference is as great as that which exists between Paul's letters to Romans and to Timothy.

Nevertheless, the theme is explained on the basis of the words which Peter uses here as contrasted to his first Epistle. The words are different, with the exception of the word *precious,* which occurs in this Epistle twice in the first chapter. Likewise, the word *faith* occurs twice in the first chapter.

The characteristic word is *knowledge* (occurring 16 times with cognate words). The epitome of the Epistle is expressed in the injunction contained in 2 Pet. 3:18, the final verse.

True gnosticism is not some esoteric information concerning a form or formula, a rite or ritual, nor is it some secret order or password. It is to know Jesus Christ as He is revealed to man in the Word of God. This is the secret of life and of Christian living (see John 17:3).

OUTLINE:

I.   **ADDITION of Christian Graces Gives Assurance, 1:1-14**
"The full knowledge of God and of Jesus our Lord" is the foundation on which Christian character is built.

II. **AUTHORITY of the Scriptures Attested by Fulfilled Prophecy,**   **1:15-21**
Scriptures give light for obedience in dark days.

III. **APOSTASY Brought in by False Teachers, ch. 2**
Church should beware of false teachers and not false prophets.

IV. **ATTITUDE Toward Return of the Lord a Test of Apostates,**   **3:1-4**

V.   **AGENDA of God for the World, 3:5-13**
1. Past World, 3:5, 6
2. Present World, 3:7-12
3. Future World, 3:13

VI. **ADMONITION to Believers, 3:14-18**
Knowledge of God's program is an incentive to grow in the knowledge of our Lord and Savior Jesus Christ.

II Peter

RECOMMENDED BOOKS:

Cramer, George H.: *First and Second Peter.*
Ironside, H. A.: *James and Peter.*
Niebor, J.: *First and Second Epistle of Peter.*
Wuest, Kenneth S.: *Second Peter in the Greek New Testament.*

I JOHN

WRITER: John the Apostle

DATE: A.D. 90-100

John evidently wrote his Gospel first, then his Epistles, and finally the book of Revelation before his death about A.D. 100.

PURPOSE:

John expressed the purpose for his writing in each of the 3 types of revelation:

His *Gospel* in John 20:30, 31

His first *Epistle* in 1 John 5:13

His *Revelation* in Rev. 1:19

Actually there is a fivefold purpose expressed in 1 John:

(1) 1:3   "That ye may have fellowship with us [other believers] and with the Father, and with his Son, Jesus Christ."
(2) 1:4   "That your joy may be full."
(3) 2:1   "That ye sin not."
(4) 5:13   "That ye may know that ye have eternal life."
(5) 5:13   "That ye may believe on the name of the Son of God."

THE FAMILY OF GOD:

This Epistle has been called the *sanctum sanctorum* of the New Testament. It takes the child of God across the threshold into the fellowship of the Father's home. It is the *family* Epistle; John is writing here to the family of God. *Father* is used 13 times, and *little children* 11 times. Paul wrote to the church; John wrote to the family. The Church is a body of believers in the position where we are blessed "with all spiritual blessings in the heavenlies in Christ." We are given that position when we believe on the Lord Jesus Christ. In the family we have a relationship which can be broken, but is restored when "we confess our sins." Then "he is faithful and just to forgive us our sins, and to cleanse us from all unrighteousness" (1 John 1:9).

The body of believers who constitute the Church are in the family of God, though the family is larger than the Church. The Church and the family are both in the kingdom of God, but are not synonymous terms.

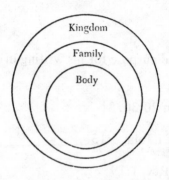

KEY WORDS:

Light (used 6 times); *love* (used 33 times); *life* (used 15 times); *fellowship* (used 4 times); *know* (used 38 times)—John wrote to meet the first heresy which entered the church. It was Gnosticism, which boasted super-knowledge. It accepted the deity of Jesus, but it denied His humanity. John gives us the true gnosticism—knowledge.

OUTLINE:

I. God is LIGHT (1:5), 1:1-2:2

    1. Prologue, 1:1, 2
    2. How the Little Children May Have Fellowship with God,
                                        1:3-2:2
        (1) By Walking in Light, 1:3-7
        (2) By Confessing Sin, 1:8-10
        (3) By Advocacy of Christ, 2:1, 2

II. God is LOVE (4:8), 2:3-4:21

1. How the Dear Children May Have Fellowship
   with Each Other *(By Walking in Love),* 2:3-14
2. The Dear Children Must Not Love the World, 2:15-28
3. How the Dear Children
   May Know Each Other and Live Together, 2:29 - 4:21
   (1) The Father's Love for His Children, 2:29-3:3
   (2) The Two Natures of the Believer in Action, 3:4-24
   (3) Warning Against False Teachers, 4:1-6
   (4) God is Love: Little Children Will Love Each Other,
   4:7-21

III. God is LIFE (5:12), ch. 5

1. Victory Over the World, 5:1-5
2. Assurance of Salvation, 5:6-21

RECOMMENDED BOOKS:

Candlish, Robert S.: *The First Epistle of John.*
Francher, Henry W.: *Fellowship with God.*
Ironside, H. A.: *The Epistles of John.*
Strauss, Lehman: *The Epistles of John.*
Thomas, W. H. Griffith: *The Apostle John.*
Vincent, Marvin R.: *Word Studies in the New Testament,* Vol. III
Vine, W. E.: *The Epistles of John.*
Wuest, Kenneth S.: *In These Last Days.* (2 Pet., 1, 2, 3 John, Jude)

II JOHN

WRITER: John the Apostle

DATE: A.D. 90-100

PERSONAL LETTER:

This Epistle is like Philemon in that it is a personal letter written by John to "the elect lady." Is the Greek word *electa* a title, or does it refer to a Christian lady in the early church by the name of Electa? It would seem that it was addressed to some lady in the church or to a local church which was extending hospitality to all those who claimed to be Christian, though some were heretics. John warns against entertaining such.

THEME: "For truth's sake"

Truth is worth contending for, and it is wrong to receive false teachers.

OUTLINE:

    I. **Love Expressed in the Boundary of Truth, vv. 1-6**
        "Love in truth"

   II. **Life is an Expression of the Doctrine of Christ, vv. 7-11**
        (False doctrine leads to evil deeds.)

 III. **Personal Greeting, vv. 12, 13**
        (False teachers are not to be received by the Christians, but true teachers are to be received with joy.)

RECOMMENDED BOOKS:

(See 1 John.)

III JOHN

WRITER: John the Apostle

DATE: A.D. 90-100

PERSONALITIES:

This is a letter similar to John's second Epistle, in that it is personal in character, and it carries the same theme of *truth*. However, this letter deals with personalities, which will be noted in the outline. In his second Epistle, John says that *truth* is worth standing for, in the third Epistle that *truth* is worth working for.

OUTLINE:

I.   **Gaius,** Beloved Brother in the Early Church, **vv. 1-8**

   (Gaius, the one to whom the letter is addressed, is urged to extend hospitality to true teachers of the Word.)

II.   **Diotrephes,** "who loves to have the preeminence," **vv.9-11**

   (Evil deeds are an expression of false doctrine.)

III.   **Demetrius** "hath good report of all men, and of the truth itself," **vv. 12-14**

   (A good life is an expression of true doctrine.)

RECOMMENDED BOOKS:

(See 1 John.)

JUDE

WRITER: Judas

Jude (this is the English form of the name *Judas*) was the brother of James (see notes on Epistle of James), and was also a half brother of the Lord Jesus Christ (Matt. 13:55).

DATE: A.D. 66-69

THEME: Assurance in days of apostasy.

The word for *keep* occurs 5 times (see vv. 1, 6, 21, 24).

REMARKS:

Jude was intending to write an epistle regarding our "common salvation," when the Spirit detoured him to write concerning the apostasy. It is a graphic and striking description of the apostasy. What was a little cloud the size of a man's hand in Jude's day is, in our day, a storm of hurricane proportions—because we are *in* the apostasy of which he foretold. It is a question now of how much worse it can become before genuine believers are taken out by the Rapture.

Jude gives the only record in the Scriptures of the contention over the body of Moses. Also, only Jude gives the prophecy of Enoch.

Jude affords a fitting introduction to the book of Revelation.

OUTLINE:

I. OCCASION of the Epistle, vv. 1-3

1. Assurance for Believers, vv. 1, 2
   (Sanctified, kept, called)
2. Change of Theme to Apostasy, v. 3

II. OCCURRENCES of Apostasy, vv. 4-16

1. Inception of Apostasy, v. 4
2. Israel in Wilderness in Unbelief Destroyed, v. 5
3. Angels Rebelled; Kept in Chains, v. 6
4. Sodom and Gomorrah Sinned
   in Sensuality; Destroyed by Fire, v. 7
5. Modern Apostate Teachers Identified, vv. 8-10
   (Despise authority)
6. Cain, Balaam, Korah Examples of Apostates, v. 11
7. Modern Apostate Teachers Defined & Described, vv. 12-16

III. OCCUPATION of Believers in Days of Apostasy, vv. 17-25

1. Believers Warned by Apostles
   That These Apostates Would Come, vv. 17-19
2. What Believers Must Do in Days of Apostasy, vv. 20-25

   (1) Build Up
   (2) Pray In
   (3) Keep Themselves
   (4) Look For
   (5) Have Compassion
   (6) Save Others
   (7) Hate Even

RECOMMENDED BOOKS:

Coder, S. Maxwell: *Jude, the Acts of the Apostates.*
Evans, Robert L.:   *The Epistle of Jude.*
Horton, T. C.:   *Outline Studies in the Epistle of Jude.*
Ironside, H. A.:   *Exposition of the Epistle of Jude.*
Wolff, Richard: *A Commentary on the Epistle of Jude.*
Wuest, Kenneth S.:   *In These Last Days.* (2 Peter, 1, 2, 3 John,
                     Jude)

REVELATION

WRITER: John the Apostle

DATE: About A.D. 95

STRIKING FEATURES:

1. It is the only prophetic book in the New Testament (in contrast to 17 prophetic books in the Old Testament).

2. John, the writer, reaches farther back into eternity past than any other writer in Scripture (John 1:1-3). He reaches farther on into eternity future in the book of Revelation.

3. Special blessing is promised the readers of this book (Rev. 1:3). Likewise, a warning is issued to those who tamper with its contents (Rev. 22:18, 19).

4. Revelation is not a sealed book (Rev. 22:10). Contrast Dan. 12:9. It is a revelation (apocalypse), which is an unveiling.

5. It is a series of visions, expressed in symbols.

6. This book is like a great union station where the great trunk lines of prophecy come in from other portions of Scripture. Revelation does not originate but consummates. It is imperative to a right understanding of the book to be able to trace each great subject of prophecy from the first reference to the terminal. There are at least 10 great subjects of prophecy which find their consummation here:

(1) The Lord Jesus Christ (Gen. 3:15)

(2) The Church (Matt. 16:18)

(3) The Resurrection and Translation of Saints
    (1 Thes. 4:13-18; 1 Cor. 15:51, 52)

(4) The Great Tribulation (Deut. 4:30, 31)

(5) Satan and Evil (Ezek. 28:11-18)

(6) The "Man of Sin" (Ezek. 28:1-10)

(7) The Course and End of Apostate Christendom
    (Dan. 2:31-45; Matt. 13)

(8) The Beginning, Course, and End of the
    "Times of the Gentiles" (Dan. 2:37; Luke 21:24)

(9) The Second Coming of Christ (Jude 14, 15)

(10) Israel's Covenants (Gen. 12:1-3)
     (Five things promised Israel)

KEY VERSES: Rev. 1:18, 19

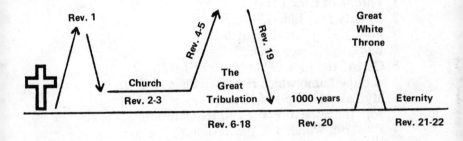

OUTLINE:

I. The PERSON of Jesus Christ—Christ in Glory, ch. 1

A. Title of the Book, 1:1
B. Method of Revelation, 1:2
C. Beatitude of Bible Study, 1:3
D. Greetings from John the Writer,
   and from Jesus Christ in Heaven, 1:4-8
E. The Post-Incarnate Christ in a Glorified Body, Judging His
   Church (the Great High Priest in the Holy of Holies), 1:9-18
   "we know him no longer after the flesh"
F. Time Division of the Contents of the Apocalypse, 1:19
G. Interpretation of the Seven Stars and Seven Lampstands, 1:20

II. The POSSESSION of Jesus Christ—The Church in the World, chs. 2, 3

A. Letter of Christ to the Church in Ephesus, 2:1-7
B. Letter of Christ to the Church in Smyrna, 2:8-11
C. Letter of Christ to the Church in Pergamum, 2:12-17
D. Letter of Christ to the Church in Thyatira, 2:18-29
E. Letter of Christ to the Church in Sardis, 3:1-6
F. Letter of Christ to the Church in Philadelphia, 3:7-13
G. Letter of Christ to the Church in Laodicea, 3:14-22

III. The PROGRAM of Jesus Christ—The Scene in Heaven, chs. 4-22

A. The Church in Heaven with Christ, chs. 4-5

"I will come again, and receive you unto myself; that where I am there ye may be also."

1. Throne of God, 4:1-3
2. Twenty-four Elders, 4:4, 5
3. Four Living Creatures, 4:6-11
4. Book with Seven Seals, 5:1-4
5. Christ: the Lion of the Tribe of Judah and the Lamb which Has Been Slain, 5:5-10
6. Myriads of Angels of Heaven Join the Song of Praise and Redemption, 5:11, 12
7. Universal Worship of the Saviour and Sovereign of the Universe, 5:13, 14

B. The Great Tribulation in the World, chs. 6-18

1. Opening of the Seven-Sealed Book, chs. 6-8:1

a. Opening of the First Seal, 6:1, 2
   (Rider on a White Horse)
b. Opening of the Second Seal, 6:3, 4
   (Rider on a Red Horse)
c. Opening of the Third Seal, 6:5, 6
   (Rider on a Black Horse)
d. Opening of the Fourth Seal, 6:7, 8
   (Rider on a Pale Horse)

e. Opening of the Fifth Seal, 6:9-11
   (Prayer of the Martyred Remnant)
f. Opening of the Sixth Seal, 6:12-17
   (The Day of Wrath Has Come—Beginning the Last Half
   of the Great Tribulation)
g. Interlude, ch. 7
  (1) Reason for the Interlude
      Between the 6th and 7th Seals, 7:1-3
  (2) Remnant of Israel Sealed, 7:4-8
  (3) Redeemed Multitude of Gentiles, 7:9-17
h. Opening of the Seventh Seal—
   Introduction of Seven Trumpets, 8:1

2. Blowing of the **Seven Trumpets,** chs. 8:2-11:19

a. Angel at the Altar with Censer of Incense, 8:2-6
b. First Trumpet—Trees Burnt, 8:7
c. Second Trumpet—Seas Become Blood, 8:8, 9
d. Third Trumpet—Fresh Water Becomes Bitter, 8:10, 11
e. Fourth Trumpet—Sun, Moon, Stars Smitten, 8:12, 13
f. Fifth Trumpet—Fallen Star and Plague of Locusts, 9:1-12
g. Sixth Trumpet—Angels Loosed
   at River Euphrates, 9:13-21
h. Interlude Between the Sixth
   and Seventh Trumpets, 10:1-11:14
  (1) The Strong Angel with the Little Book, 10:1-7
  (2) John Eats the Little Book, 10:8-11
  (3) Date for the Ending of
      "The Times of the Gentiles," 11:1, 2
  (4) Duration of the Prophesying
      of the Two Witnesses, 11:3-12
  (5) Doom of the Second Woe—
      Great Earthquake, 11:13, 14
i. Seventh Trumpet—End of Great Tribulation
   and Opening of Temple in Heaven, 11:15-19

3. Seven Performers During the Great Tribulation, chs. 12-13

a. The Woman—Israel, 12:1, 2
b. The Red Dragon—Satan, 12:3, 4
c. The Child of the Woman—Jesus Christ, 12:5, 6
d. Michael, the Archangel, Wars with the Dragon, 12:7-12

e. The Dragon Persecutes the Woman, 12:13-16
f. Remnant of Israel, 12:17
g. Wild Beast Out of the Sea—
   a Political Power and a Person, 13:1-10
 (1) Wild Beast, Description, 13:1, 2
 (2) Wild Beast, Death Dealing Stroke, 13:3
 (3) Wild Beast, Deity Assumed, 13:4, 5
 (4) Wild Beast, Defying God, 13:6-8
 (5) Wild Beast, Defiance Denied to Anyone, 13:9, 10
h. Wild Beast Out of the Earth—
   a Religious Leader, 13:11-18
 (1) Wild Beast, Description, 13:11
 (2) Wild Beast, Delegated Authority, 13:12-14
 (3) Wild Beast, Delusion Perpetrated
     on the World, 13:15-17
 (4) Wild Beast, Designation, 13:18

4. Looking to the End of the Great Tribulation, ch. 14

a. Picture of the Lamb with the 144,000, 14:1-5
b. Proclamation of the Everlasting Gospel, 14:6, 7
c. Pronouncement of Judgment on Babylon, 14:8
d. Pronouncement of Judgment on
   Those Who Received the Mark of the Beast, 14:9-12
e. Praise for Those Who Die in the Lord, 14:13
f. Preview of Armageddon, 14:14-20

5. Pouring Out of the
Seven Mixing Bowls of Wrath, chs. 15, 16
a. Preparation for Final Judgment
   of the Great Tribulation, 15:1-16:1
 (1) Tribulation Saints in Heaven
     Worship God Because He is Holy and Just, 15:1-4
 (2) Temple of the Tabernacle Opened in Heaven that
     Seven Angels, Having Seven Golden Bowls, Might
     Proceed Forth,   15:5-16:1
b. Pouring Out of the First Bowl, 16:2
c. Pouring Out of the Second Bowl, 16:3
d. Pouring Out of the Third Bowl, 16:4-7
e. Pouring Out of the Fourth Bowl, 16:8, 9
f. Pouring Out of the Fifth Bowl, 16:10, 11
g. Pouring Out of the Sixth Bowl, 16:12

h. Interlude: Kings of Inhabited Earth
  Proceed to Har-Magedon, 16:13-16
i. Pouring Out of the Seventh Bowl, 16:17-21

6. The **Two Babylons Judged,** chs. 17, 18

a. The Apostate Church in the Great Tribulation, ch. 17
  (1) Great Harlot Riding the Wild Beast, 17:1-7
  (2) Wild Beast Destroys the Great Harlot, 17:8-18
  (3) Anticipation of Joy in Heaven
    Because of Judgment on Babylon, 18:20-24

C. Marriage of the Lamb and Return of Christ in Judgment,
                                                    ch. 19

1. Four Hallelujahs, 19:1-6
2. Bride of the Lamb and Marriage Supper, 19:7-10
3. Return of Christ as
  King of Kings and Lord of Lords, 19:11-16
4. Battle of Armageddon, 19:17, 18
5. Hell Opened, 19:19-21

D. Millennium, ch. 20

1. Satan Bound 1,000 Years, 20:1-3
2. Saints of the Great Tribulation
  Reign with Christ 1,000 Years, 20:4-6
3. Satan Loosed After 1,000 Years, 20:7-9
4. Satan Cast Into Lake of Fire and Brimstone, 20:10
5. Setting of Great White Throne Where Lost Are Judged and
  Follow Satan Into Lake of Fire and Brimstone, 20:11-15

E. Entrance into Eternity; Eternity Unveiled, chs. 21, 22

1. New Heaven, New Earth, New Jerusalem, 21:1, 2
2. New Era, 21:3-8
3. New Jerusalem,
  Description of the Eternal Abode of the Bride, 21:9-21
4. New Relationship—God Dwelling with Man, 21:22, 23
5. New Center of the New Creation, 21:24-27
6. River of the Water of Life and Tree of Life, 22:1-5

7. Promise of Return of Christ, 22:6-16
8. Final Invitation and Warning, 22:17-19
9. Final Promise and Prayer, 22:20, 21

RECOMMENDED BOOKS:

DeHaan, M. R.: *Revelation.*
Govett, Robert: *The Apocalypse Expounded by Scripture.*
Ironside, H. A.: *Lectures on the Book of Revelation.*
McGee, J. Vernon: *Reveling Through Revelation,* Vols. 1 & 2
Newell, William R.: *The Book of the Revelation.*
Pentecost, J. Dwight: *Things To Come.*
Seiss, J. A.: *The Apocalypse, Lectures on the Book of Revelation.*
Strauss, Lehman: *The Book of the Revelation.*
Vincent, Marvin: *Word Studies in the New Testament.*
Walvoord, John F.: *The Revelation.*

SAMPLE SUMMARY FOR EACH CHAPTER

1. Theme of Chapter—

2. Most Important Verse—

3. Most Prominent Word—

4. Teaching about Christ—

5. Command to Obey—

6. Promise to Claim—

7. New Truth Learned—

Job, Psalms, Proverbs, Ecclesiastes, Song of Solom
and Lamentations (Poetical Books)